# 50 Interviews: Successful Property Managers

*Advice and Winning Strategies from Industry Leaders*

**VOLUME 2 (EPISODES 26-50)**

by Michael Levy

**Wise Media Group**
Denver, CO

**50 Interviews: Successful Property Managers (Vol. 2)**
Copyright © 2010 by Michael Levy
http://www.SuccessfulPropertyManagers.com

ISBN #: 978-1-935689-02-7

Published by
Wise Media Group
444 17th Street, Suite 507
Denver, CO 80202
www.WiseMediaGroup.com

All rights reserved. No part of this book may be reproduced in any form or by any electronic or mechanical means, including information storage and retrieval systems, without written permission from the author, except in the case of a reviewer, who may quote brief passages embodied in critical articles or in a review.

Trademarked names appear throughout this book. Rather than use a trademark symbol with every occurrence of a trademarked name, names are used in an editorial fashion, with no intention of infringement of the respective owner's trademark.

The information in this book is distributed on an "as is" basis, without warranty. Although every precaution has been taken in the preparation of this work, neither the author nor the publisher shall have any liability to any person or entity with respect to any loss or damage caused or alleged to be caused directly or indirectly by the information contained in this book.

First edition.
Printed in the United States of America.

Volume purchase discounts are available. Please visit www.50interviews.com for more information.

*This book is dedicated to my wife, Cathy, and my two lovely daughters, Chelsea and Rebecca. If it were not for their tremendous support and love, this book would not have been possible. I love them all dearly!*

# ACKNOWLEDGEMENTS

When I started out on this journey to write a book, I had no idea how much effort it would take. There were so many people that contributed, and without their help, this book would never have been completed.

So, I would like to sincerely thank the following people:

The 25 property managers who agreed to give their valuable time to do the interviews with me and to offer their help in anyway I needed: Joy Anzalone, Nancy Ashmore, Bennett Borsuk, Raymond Callahan, Noreen Daly-Norris, James Donnelly, Marc Einhorn, Stephen Francis, Vickie Gaskill, Samuel Goldstein, Philip Henderson, Trevor Henson, Charlie Koons, Joseph Lacko, Beth Machen, Andrea Martini, Julie Muir, Russell Munz, Patti Oriot, Michael Prochelo, Mark Quinn, Kellie Sanders, Bob Spicker, Edward Thomas, and Nigel Worrall.

A special thanks to Patti Oriot and Trevor Henson who not only gave their time to be an interviewee but also contributed very valuable content for the two appendices at the end of this book.

Thank you also, to Aimee Miller, vice president of marketing at AppFolio, Inc. in Goleta, California, who provided significant assistance and encouragement for this book.

Bob and Lucille Steiner for their encouragement, support, and feedback on some of the initial book cover designs.

My family, friends, and colleagues who have given me so much support, inspiration, and encouragement throughout the entire process of publishing this book. And also my business partners in my three businesses: Prue Kaley, my partner with NorthernColoradoRentals.com, LLC, Mike Robichaud, my partner with NoCoAds, and Cathy Hettleman, my partner with Levy Consulting, LLC.

My fellow board members of the Northern Colorado Rental Housing Association (NoCoRHA) who have provided me with tremendous education on the property management industry: Robert Miller, Anna Barbre, Melissa Emerson, Dick Eshelman, Kris Farnsworth, Paul Farrer, Carrie Gillis, Belinda Kernaghan, Jeannie Ortega, Beverly Perina, Stephanie Schilling, Sandy Shoen, and Robert Valois.

The numerous transcribers, editors, and layout specialists that helped pulled all the pieces together for this book; Betsy Osgood, Veronica Yager, Tiffany Garofalo, Erin Stettler, and Nick Zelinger.

My very supportive mother, Harriet Levy, as well as my father, Donald Levy who taught me much of what I now know about property management. Through his help and coaching I have been able to effectively manage a number of my own rental properties (residential and vacation) for the last 25+ years. My two brothers David Levy and Rick Levy. David, a partner with Levy, Erlanger & Company, CPAs in San Francisco, California, founded his company in 1986 for the purpose of providing high-quality financial services to California community associations. Rick is the chief financial officer with SCOLR Pharma, Inc. in Bothell, Washington.

And last, but certainly not least, a million thank you's to Brian Schwartz, the founder and publisher of the 50 Interviews brand. Brian has been an incredible person to work with. His support, inspiration, and tireless enthusiasm have been invaluable to me throughout the entire process.

There are countless more individuals, that although I may not have mentioned them here, I am ever grateful to each and every one of them for their contributions to the creation of this book.

# TABLE OF CONTENTS

Introduction .................................................................................. i

Joy Anzalone, Burton Carol Management, LLC ................................. 1

Nancy Ashmore, Cagan Management ................................................ 7

Bennett Borsuk, The Cabrio Group ................................................... 13

Raymond Callahan, Spruce Hill Property Services ........................... 19

Noreen Daly-Norris, Century 21 Cardinal Realty .............................. 25

James Donnelly, Castle Group .......................................................... 31

Marc Einhorn, Capitol Management ................................................ 37

Stephen Francis, Pristine Property Management of
  Martha's Vineyard ........................................................................ 43

Vickie Gaskill, Bell Anderson Associates, LLC ................................... 49

Samuel Goldstein, Galman Group ..................................................... 55

Philip Henderson, Henderson Properties, Inc. .................................. 61

Trevor Henson, First Light Property Management, Inc. .................... 67

Charlie Koons, Mountain-n-Plains Real Estate Services, Inc. ............ 73

Joseph Lacko, JL Management ......................................................... 79

Beth Machen, Machen Advisory Group ............................................ 85

Andrea Martini, Midland Realty and Development ......................... 91

Julie Muir, Elliott Associates, Inc. ..................................................... 97

Russell Munz, Pyramid Real Estate Group ...................................... 103

Patti Oriot, Maui Markets ............................................................... 109

Michael Prochelo, Financial Management Group ........................... 115

Mark Quinn, Banyan Property Management, Inc. .......................... 119

Kellie Sanders, Village Green ........................................................... 125

Bob Spicker, Colliers International .................................................. 131

Edward Thomas, Property Management People, Inc. .................... 137

Nigel Worrall, Florida Leisure Vacation Homes .............................. 143

Appendix D:
  Basic Marketing Tips for Vacation Rentals,
  Patti Oriot .................................................................................. 149

Appendix E:
  Online Marketing and Social Media for Property Management,
  Trevor Henson ........................................................................... 155

About the Author ............................................................................ 165

# INTRODUCTION

In late 2009, I embarked on this journey to write a book about successful property managers. My goal was to pull together valuable advice, tips, and winning strategies from some of the most successful property managers in the country. The targeted reader audience are both individuals considering property management as a career option, as well as veteran property managers interested in learning from other successful property managers in the industry.

This book, Volume II, is a collection of interviews with 25 property managers from across the United States specializing in commercial property management, community association management, residential property management, and management of vacation rentals. Although there are many commonalities among the interviewees, there is also a vast array of unique approaches that are described throughout the interviews.

One common theme was the importance of networking and belonging to some of the most successful organizations in the property management industry, specifically the National Association of Residential Property Managers (NARPM), the Institute of Real Estate Management (IREM), and the National Apartment Association (NAA) were mentioned more than any others. The importance of good communication and people interaction skills were also mentioned quite often. With respect to the biggest challenges being faced by property managers, the economy was a clear stand out. What was most interesting is how everyone looked at the challenges from a different perspective and dealt with the issues in different ways. I was also fascinated by the diversity of answers to the question related to what they looked for in their employees.

I had a great time doing the interviews and editing them into this Volume II edition.

Volume I (published in February 2010) was a collection of interviews with another 25 property managers specializing in residential property management.

It is not possible to include the complete content of all the interviews in this book, so I have started a blog for those interested in reading more about these successful property managers. You may visit the blog at www.SuccessfulPropertyManagers.com. I will also include many other additional resources for property managers including discussion forums, tips and advice for property managers as well as individual landlords, property management news, and much more.

# 26

*"Solid foundations, solid people."*
Joy Anzalone, Burton Carol Management, LLC

**BACKGROUND**
Joy Anzalone lives in Bratenahl, Ohio. Joy has been with Burton Carol Management, LLC for over 28 years and is currently the chief operating officer. The company has 200 employees and manages 25 properties in Michigan, Ohio, and Florida. Their portfolio consists of a resort hotel, two successful restaurants, commercial buildings such as strip retail centers, and 5,000 multi-family apartment units.

**INTERVIEW**
**Q:** How did you get into property management?
**A:** I'd graduated from college and was about to marry my high school sweetheart when my mother passed away. I was too heartbroken to start a job search, so my husband took an on-site maintenance job at one of the company's properties. Out of desperation I took a job in housekeeping, never realizing where that could lead. Five years and five promotions later, I was asked to take over the company's apartment division, which at that time, had 18,000 units in four states.

**Q:** Did you have a mentor at the time?
**A:** My greatest mentor is William Burton Risman, who was chairman of the company board when I met him in 1982. At the time, I was a housekeeper at my first property, a hotel located on the entrance to an interstate. The ravine close by was filled with trash, and I volunteered to go down and clean up the glass, bottles, and cans. While I was working in the

rain and the wind, a big Cadillac drove up. The driver looked at me, opened the door, and climbed down the steep incline into the gully. He had no idea who I was, but he shook my hand and thanked me for cleaning the front of his property! I felt like a million bucks and believed at that moment that I could do anything. A few years later he took me under his wing and taught me the true art of making all associates feel as special as I did on that rainy day.

Q: What educational classes have you taken along the way?
A: I graduated from Kent State University with a major in journalism and a minor in criminal justice. I've gone to countless seminars, am certified in fair housing, and stay current on all areas of property management. I have also taught many training and motivational classes for management companies, including my own.

Q: How do you keep up with all of the laws that affect your property management business?
A: I go to seminars offered by the law firms that we do business with, read every possible periodical that I can, and I'm very active with the local apartment association, serving on the executive committee and as a past president.

Q: Are there any books that you would recommend?
A: *The One Minute Manager* as well as *Who Moved My Cheese?*, both by Kenneth Blanchard and Spencer Johnson. Also, *Leadership is an Art* by Max Depree, *One Page Management* by Riaz Khadem and Robert Lorber, Steven Covey's *Seven Habits of Highly Effective People*, *The Wisdom of Teams* by Jon Katzenbach and Douglas Smith, and *Beyond Basketball* by Mike Krzyzewski.

Q: Do you belong to any other professional associations?
A: I've been very active in the Northeast Ohio Apartment Association for more than a decade, as a member of several committees. I also belong to the Condo Association Board

and a homeowners' association board.

**Q:** How do you use the Internet in your property management business?

**A:** It's how we do business now, in so many ways. Our property management company is web based, so we work in real time, all the time. The Internet is how new associates and customers find us, it's our source of advertising, and it's how we order supplies. We stay on top of every aspect of our business, 24/7 and even "after hours," down to monitoring our boilers and other large equipment.

**Q:** Are there any slogans that your company uses?

**A:** Our tagline for our company is: "Solid foundations, solid people." I also live by "There are no good deals with bad people," and "I would rather have you try and fail, than not try at all." My mentor in this business drummed these things into my head, and they are as true today as they were 25 years ago.

**Q:** What do you attribute your success to?

**A:** I am incredibly blessed with an amazing team of people who make me look good. My keys to success, without question, were the opportunities given to me by William Burton Risman and Rob Risman, who showed me how to care, be fair, but demand and expect the best out of people. My parents taught me to work hard, to be true to my word always, and to be appreciative of everything. And my wonderful husband has always encouraged me. Every time a challenge came my way he told me, "You can do this."

> **MY PARENTS INSTILLED THE VALUES IN ME TO WORK HARD, BE TRUE TO MY WORD ALWAYS, NEVER DEPEND ON ANYONE FOR ANYTHING BUT MYSELF, AND TO BE APPRECIATIVE OF EVERYTHING.**

Q: How do you attract and retain the best employees?
A: You must lead by example every day, treat everyone as you would like to be treated, and have great communication. There has to be a balance between working on problems and compliments on a job well done, so that employees appreciate constructive feedback and the chance to do a better job. I take pride in the fact that we have tremendous longevity at our company.

Q: What are the most important attributes you look for in an employee?
A: The number one thing is attitude. I can teach you every part of this job except for that. Employees must be great team players who are willing to go the extra mile, and be honest, genuinely good human beings.

Q: What are some of the biggest challenges you face and how are you overcoming those challenges?
A: We have a great operation but the difficult market has created challenges: tenants are losing jobs, markets are experiencing negative growth, and vacancies are a big issue. We are talented negotiators, leveraging our purchasing power and our great payment record to keep costs down and take good care of our properties. You are only in this business today if you have a passion for it and can see past difficulties to better times in the future.

> WE ATTRACT AND RETAIN THE BEST EMPLOYEES THROUGH GREAT COMMUNICATION AND BY TREATING EVERYBODY THE WAY WE WANT TO BE TREATED.

Q: What do you find the most rewarding about property management?
A: I love what I do, and the company my coworkers and I have created together. It's rewarding to mentor people and earn the respect of my peers in the business. I love to take a prop-

erty that is failing and turn it around.

**Q:** What do you see as some of the biggest opportunities for new property managers getting into the industry?

**A:** This is the greatest business in the whole wide world. Anyone with the right attitude, who works hard and is in the right organization, can succeed. This has become the era of asset management and making sure properties optimize their potential. Everyone is having a tough time, but successful property managers will leave no stone unturned to produce returns for owners and retain tenants. Managing well is key. This has always been the case but today it means the difference between being in business or being out of business. Plain and simple!

> **VACANCIES ARE A BIG ISSUE. MY GREATEST CHALLENGE RIGHT NOW IS DEALING WITH RESIDENTS WHO ARE LOSING THEIR JOBS.**

*"Our greatest weakness lies in giving up. The most certain way to succeed is always to try just one more time."*

-Thomas Edison

# 27

*"Keep it objective and be transparent. Don't get caught in the middle of a dispute between a board member and an owner."*
                    Nancy Ashmore, Cagan Management

**BACKGROUND**

Nancy Ashmore lives in Harwood Heights, Illinois. Nancy was formerly a portfolio manager at Cagan Management. At the time, the company employed about 50 people and had about 300 clients. When Nancy was at Cagan, she managed condominiums, apartments, co-ops, and town homes. Her specialty was community associations.

**INTERVIEW**

**Q:** How did you get into property management?

**A:** My husband and I were building engineers in the late 1990s, when the conversion of apartment buildings to condominiums really began. The condo owners trusted us to know their buildings well, and we would get requests to attend their board meetings. I could see the coming demand for property managers specializing in community management, and decided to follow that career path.

**Q:** When you started to get into property management, did you have a mentor?

**A:** My mentor was Michael Daniels of Cagan Management Group.[1] If I had a problem, he was there, and he taught me a lot: be decisive, keep things simple, look at the big picture, and periodically take a step back.

**Q:** What educational classes have you taken that have been particularly valuable to you?

A: I did all the coursework to obtain my real estate broker and associate residential appraiser licenses. Those courses laid a solid foundation for me to build on. I joined the Community Association Institute (CAI) and Institute of Real Estate Management (IREM). Both offer excellent coursework and designation programs for real estate professionals concentrating on property management.

> **EVERY PROPERTY MANAGER NEEDS TO READ ROBERT'S RULES OF ORDER, OR AT LEAST THE CLIFFSNOTES VERSION.**

Q: How do you keep up with the various laws that affect your property management business?

A: Local government, fire and police departments, village halls, legal services, building engineers and contractors are a wealth of information. They typically have websites that post zoning and building codes, legal bulletins and the like. Other property managers also readily share their firsthand experiences dealing with new codes and enforcement.

Q: Are there any books that have been particularly valuable to you?

A: Every property manager needs to read *Robert's Rules of Order*, or at least the CliffsNotes version. Robert's rules can guide you on conducting an effective board meeting, keeping everyone pleasant and polite. IREM's *Journal of Property Management* is a good source for staying on top of new products and legislation; CAI publishes magazine articles written by managers, board members and homeowners. Some are funny, but always a good lesson learned.

Q: Any other associations that you belong to?

A: The Chicago Apartment Association has been a successful marketing tool for me.

**Q:** How does your company use the Internet for your property management business?
**A:** They use it for e-mail and to post association rules, regulations, and resale documents. People can look online for an apartment or to pay their assessments.

**Q:** Do you know if they still use traditional advertising, like newspapers?
**A:** Absolutely; they manage a lot of rental properties, so their rental ads get their company name out there. They also advertise in trade journals and have an informative DVD film that introduces their management services.

**Q:** Does the company use Craigslist for advertising rental properties?
**A:** Yes, but you have to be careful with Craigslist, as with any web-based services.

**Q:** What do you attribute your success to?
**A:** It's a lot of hard work, being very dedicated to the field, and keeping up with my education because you never stop learning in this business. And also, just loving what I do.

**Q:** When things aren't going too well, where do you draw your strength or inspiration from?
**A:** Sometimes I have to take a step back, spend some quality time with the family, pick up a good book or take a course, and that rejuevnates me. I'll tell myself to get out there and apply what I've just learned – it brings my confidence back and gives me a fresh start.

> **I ATTRIBUTE MY SUCCESS TO A LOT OF HARD WORK, BEING VERY DEDICATED TO THE FIELD, AND ALWAYS LEARNING.**

**Q:** Do you have any particular slogans that you or your company uses?

**A:** The company always emphasized: "Be proactive, not reactive." In other words, don't wait for the calls and complaints to come in or the roof to fall down. Do a site visit, catch things before they happen, practice good finance and budget planning. One of my slogans is: "Keep it objective and be transparent." There are no secrets and you shouldn't be afraid to tell your association anything. You never want to get caught in the middle of a dispute between a board member and an owner.

> **THE MOST IMPORTANT ATTRIBUTES FOR AN EMPLOYEE ARE A STRONG EDUCATIONAL BACKGROUND AND VERY STRONG PROBLEM SOLVING SKILLS.**

**Q:** What are the most important attributes you look for in an employee?
**A:** Cagan looks for people with a strong educational background, flexibility, and very good creative problem solving skills.

**Q:** What did you do in your property management business that you wish you had started doing sooner?
**A:** I probably gave my associations too much information. I would collect any bit of information on a property that I could, read all their documents and meeting minutes' history. After a board meeting, I wouldn't hear from the members for weeks because I was giving them too much to process at one time. I should have kept it short and simple, dealt with the concerns at hand. The quality of the information is more important than the quantity.

**Q:** What are some of the biggest mistakes that you see new property managers making?
**A:** New property mangers are a little shy when it comes to communication with the boards, but they really need to keep it flowing. They should do weekly updates or send a quick note to keep the members up on the status of what they're work-

ing on, and never tell a client that they are too busy; that sends up a red flag.

**Q:** What are some of the biggest challenges you had?

**A:** In a tough economy and real estate market, we have faced more and more foreclosures on condominiums. Each one hurts the association; it's one less assessment coming in. At the trade shows and seminars now, it's all about dealing with collections and trying to function with fewer on-time assessments being paid.

**Q:** How do you deal with that?

**A:** You have to have a really good collections attorney, and be proactive. When you see a "For Sale" sign on the door, it's time to get the realtor's name, check the county's Recorder of Deeds or local MLS directory, and find out whether the owner or the bank has legal title. Then you establish communications with whoever has possession, and serve proper notice to collect the debt.

> **KEEP IT SHORT AND SIMPLE. DON'T OVERWHELM THE BOARDS WITH TOO MUCH INFORMATION TO PROCESS.**

**Q:** Did you have any tips or tricks to avoid repeating the same mistakes?

**A:** Again, you have to be proactive, and learn from your mistakes. Maybe you sent out a manager's report to the board and got a lot of negative feedback on it. You may need to look at the report and figure out how you could have worded it in a more positive light, or perhaps just reiterate existing rules and regulations and try again.

**Q:** What do you find is the most rewarding aspect of your property management business?

**A:** Nobody's going to pat you on the back and say, "Hey, you did a nice job." You usually only hear about the bad things, and in the beginning the association constantly challenges you. When they stop challenging you and start working with you as a team, you know you've earned their trust. That makes the job so much easier and very rewarding.

Q: Describe for me what your best association would look like.
A: Community living has its positives and its negatives: all the rules, regulations, and procedures everyone has to go through to get things done. The best association is one in which everybody understands their role and responsibilities, so there's a lot more teamwork and a lot less distrust.

Q: What are some of the biggest opportunities you see for new property managers?
A: It's a business that is pretty much recession-proof; no matter where you go, your skills will be needed. Right now, our newest clients are the banks which have a legal interest in, and responsibility for, the properties they've foreclosed on. Banks rely upon good managers to help keep those properties maintained, so there is opportunity to gain clients even in this tough economic environment.

> **IT'S A BUSINESS THAT IS PRETTY MUCH RECESSION-PROOF.**

---

[1] See Volume I for an interview with Michael Daniels.

# 28

*"You get out of life what you put into it.
Put more in."*
Bennett Borsuk, The Cabrio Group

◆

**BACKGROUND**
Bennett Borsuk lives in Ann Arbor, Michigan, and has been in the property management business for 10 years. He is a partner with The Cabrio Group, which was established in 2006. The company has six employees and manages 15 properties consisting of office, retail, and multi-family buildings (mostly housing for University of Michigan students).

**INTERVIEW**
**Q:** How did you get started in property management and did you have a mentor at the time?
**A:** While I was attending the University of Michigan in Ann Arbor, I bought my first apartment building on campus. That got my interest going and everything grew from there. My father was my mentor at the time.

**Q:** Have you taken any educational classes that you have found to be particularly valuable to you?
**A:** I attend various national conferences, seminars and other events, all of which have been pretty informative and valuable. I also take the classes that the state of Michigan requires for renewal of your real estate broker's license.

**Q:** How do you keep up with all the laws that affect the property management industry?
**A:** I keep up by networking with all the people I know in the business, by attending seminars, and through my real estate

continuing education.

Q: Which organizations put on some good conferences?
A: A good organization is the Certified Commercial Investment Member (CCIM) Institute, which does a lot of education in the commercial realm.

Q: Are there any websites that you would recommend as good resources?
A: I use GlobeSt.com and CCIM.com.

Q: What do you attribute your success to?
A: I attribute it to hard work, integrity, resourcefulness, and a lot of time invested in finding creative ways to solve problems.

Q: When things don't go particularly well, from where do you draw your inspiration and strength?
A: It takes a lot of effort to get through the bad times, but you have to stay optimistic. Things do get better; it's just a matter of time.

Q: Do you have any slogans that you use?
A: "You get out of life what you put into it. Put more in."

Q: How do you attract and retain the best employees?
A: We have very high standards for performance and work ethic, and we reward employees well for excellence.

Q: What is the most important attribute that you look for in an employee?
A: We look for employees who are self-driven and have an entrepreneurial spirit. A lot of the problems you come across in this business don't have cut-and-dried solutions. You have to be

> **TWO GOOD WEBSITE RESOURCES ARE GLOBEST.COM AND CCIM.COM.**

creative and think outside the box.

**Q:** What are some of the biggest mistakes that you see new property managers making?
**A:** A lot of them get into property management with little education or experience, and try to grow too big too quickly, not truly understanding what it takes to be in this business. They should keep things small, and grow slowly and steadily.

**Q:** What are some of the biggest challenges that you face in your company and how are you overcoming those challenges?
**A:** The poor economy and external market factors like declining rental rates and property values make things difficult. We're trying to be more creative as we structure deals and find solutions that are beneficial for everyone involved.

**Q:** What do you do to make sure you don't make the same mistakes again?
**A:** Making mistakes is just part of life, and we use that as a learning experience; we'll modify our various procedures and policies if necessary to avoid making the same mistakes. We also take the time to learn everything we can about the buildings we run. The more we know about a building, the better off we will be.

> **WE LOOK FOR EMPLOYEES WITH AN ENTREPRENEURIAL SPIRIT, WHO ARE SELF-DRIVEN, AND HAVE THE ABILITY TO THINK OUTSIDE THE BOX.**

**Q:** Describe for me your best client.
**A:** Our corporate philosophy is that all our clients are our best clients, and we treat them accordingly.

**Q:** What is the most rewarding aspect of your property management business?
**A:** The most rewarding thing is to provide a quality space for

someone, whether it's a place to live, or a place to start a new business – we want everyone to be successful.

**Q:** What are some of the biggest opportunities for new property managers?
**A:** There will continue to be a lot of opportunities for new managers. They should take advantage of the current economic conditions and find imaginative ways to manage distressed properties for existing and new clients.

**Q:** Can you contrast for me some of the differences within residential property management, between student housing and non-student housing?
**A:** Student housing is definitely much more management-intensive, especially when it comes to maintenance! You deal with a lot of students who have never lived on their own before. They don't know how to change a light bulb or plunge a toilet, and tend to lock themselves out of their apartments. But one of the big advantages with student leasing is that it's a very stable market, regardless of economic conditions.

**Q:** Are contracts and lease agreements more custom on the commercial side and more standard on the residential side?
**A:** Definitely! Residential leases are very simple and short. They're typically for a year term with a total lease of perhaps $13,000. Commercial leases can be much more comprehensive documents, upwards of 70 pages long, and you usually deal with larger dollar figures as well. An office lease, for example, might have a five-year term at two million dollars.

> **THE MOST REWARDING THING IS TO PROVIDE A SPACE FOR SOMEONE WHO'S GOING TO START A NEW BUSINESS, AND TO SEE HIM MAKE IT A SUCCESS.**

**Q:** Do you use a real estate lawyer on the commercial side?
**A:** We have a couple of attorneys who do lease reviews and fi-

nalize the documents before they're put into effect.

*"Many of life's failures are people who did not realize how close they were to success when they gave up."*
                                                    -Thomas Edison

# 29

*"Our best association is one that wants to work together for the common good of everybody."*
Raymond Callahan, Spruce Hill Property Services

**BACKGROUND**
Raymond Callahan lives in West Springfield, Massachusetts, and has been in the property management business since 1971. He is the president of Spruce Hill Property Services, which has 12 employees and manages 13 condominium associations ranging in size from eight to 120 units.

**INTERVIEW**
**Q:** How did you get into property management?
**A:** I was kind of forced into it from the time I bought a two-family home in 1971; then we built the business by buying more units over the next 14 years. In the mid-1980s we sold our properties and took a year off to travel. I returned to the industry by getting into condo association management.

**Q:** Are there any classes that you found to be particularly valuable to you?
**A:** The Institute of Real Estate Management (IREM) has a lot of excellent classes. The ones I took go back to IREM's beginnings in the 1980s.

**Q:** How do you keep up with all the various laws that affect your property management business?
**A:** I get a lot of information from IREM and, as a realtor, I get updates and information from the Board of Realtors as well. Our attorneys send out regular newsletters that keep us updated on different issues and laws in the property manage-

ment industry.

**Q:** What associations do you belong to?
**A:** The Community Associations Institute (CAI) and IREM for property management are both very good.

**Q:** How do you use the Internet for your property management business?
**A:** Originally, computers were supposed to help you cut back on paperwork and that certainly turned out not to be the case; it's a lot more. Access to information is now much more readily available, but instant access can present new problems. With smart phones, for example, everyone wants instant access to you all the time.

**Q:** Do you still use any traditional advertising, like newspapers?
**A:** We've never done much advertising, to be perfectly honest. Ninety-nine percent of our "advertising" is by word of mouth. The other one percent is the sign on our trucks, which people see on the road.

**Q:** What do you attribute your success to?
**A:** It's due to hard work; there's no getting out of it. This is a business that requires you to be on call 24 hours a day, seven days a week, 365 days a year. Many holidays have been cut short because of this job.

**Q:** When things aren't going particularly well, from where do you draw your strength and inspiration?
**A:** You just have to know that what you are doing is correct. I've always felt that our job is to identify our clientele and what they are looking for. There are associations of different types and the demand levels for each of them are quite different. The trustees or directors are the ones you're working for directly, and they call the shots,

> **CAI AND IREM ARE BOTH VERY GOOD ORGANIZATIONS.**

but the unit owners ultimately control everything. Our job is to manage our associations with everybody's best interest at heart.

**Q:** Are there any slogans that you or your company operates by?
**A:** "Treat everybody the way you want to be treated."

**Q:** How do you attract and retain the best employees?
**A:** You have to understand people's strengths and weaknesses and use them the best way you can. You must be fair and honest about your expectations, and remember that nobody is perfect.

**Q:** What's the most important attribute you look for in an employee?
**A:** General appearance and overall competence are key.

**Q:** What are you doing now in property management that you feel you should have done sooner?
**A:** I probably should have gotten a certification, or gone to college for a degree. Once you are in business long enough and build a reputation, it's a non-issue, but it probably would have opened doors for me that I had to otherwise fight to get through.

> **NINETY-NINE PERCENT OF OUR ADVERTISING IS BY WORD OF MOUTH.**

**Q:** What are the biggest mistakes you see new property managers making?
**A:** I don't think they understand the time commitment that is required and typically won't put up with the hours, which are going to get worse, not better. I'm in the office by 6:30 a.m. and sometimes I don't get home until 9:30 p.m. because of association board meetings.

**Q:** What are some of the biggest challenges that you face?

**A:** Homeowners associations are usually under-funded, so their biggest challenges are financial in general. Members don't always understand what things cost, that roofs have a shelf life and will need to be replaced. They also tend to focus on current issues, and forget to build reserve funds to plan for tomorrow's expenses.

**Q:** What about for your business, what kind of challenges are you facing there?

**A:** One challenge is employee training and retention, which seems specifically true for field maintenance staff. Often we train them and then they either go off on their own, or find other jobs.

**Q:** Do you have any tips or tricks that have helped you to avoid repeating the same mistakes?

**A:** We're unique in that we have our own general maintenance crew and keep as much work in-house as we can to oversee responsibility for it. With our landscaping and snow removal crews for example, we can do 90% of all the maintenance for our associations, and have our employees on-site almost every day.

**Q:** Describe for me your best client.

**A:** Any association that works together for everyone's common good is a "best client." We can argue, have discussions, compliment each other or disagree, but everybody is basically on the same page and it's never a question of "us against them." One of our associations has run like this for 10 years and we've never had harsh words. On the other hand, some associations are impossible.

> **OUR BIGGEST CHALLENGES ARE EMPLOYEE RETENTION AND GETTING PEOPLE TRAINED.**

**Q:** What have been the most rewarding aspects of your property management business?

**A:** I am self-employed and can pretty much call my own shots. I can take time off if I need to, because I have employees whom I feel very confident with, and can trust.

**Q:** What do you see as some of the biggest opportunities for new property managers?

**A:** There are now more condos being built, and more homeowners associations being formed, than ever before. They'll have lots of problems and challenges for new property managers to come in and fix.

*"Success consists of getting up just one more time than you fall."*
-Oliver Goldsmith

# 30

*"Every day is a challenge and a reward."*
Noreen Daly-Norris, Century 21 Cardinal Realty

### BACKGROUND
Noreen Daly-Norris lives in Stafford, Virginia. She is the property manager for Century 21 Cardinal Realty and oversees 40 to 60 properties, including private homes, town homes, and condos. Noreen has been in the industry for 20 years.

### INTERVIEW
**Q:** How did you get into property management, and did you have a mentor at the time?

**A:** I took a job as a receptionist at a property close to our home. Six months later I was the assistant director. Six months after that I was the director.

**Q:** Any educational classes that you have taken that have been particularly valuable to you?

**A:** I took classes through the Building Owners and Managers Association (BOMA) and got my Real Property Administrator (RPA) designation; these were very well-rounded and difficult courses. In property management you are dealing not just with buildings, but with people, accounting, landscaping, construction issues, air, land, and environmental issues. You really have to be able to juggle all of those things.

**Q:** How do you keep up with all the laws that affect your property management business?

**A:** I keep a current copy of *Law for Management*, and when in doubt I go online to the Virginia state housing website. I can check property management law there and make sure that I'm being accurate and legal.

**Q:** How do you use the Internet in your property management business?

**A:** I'm out of my office most of the time, doing showings, solving problems, and meeting with owners or tenants. I need to advertise as quickly and efficiently as possible, which is where the Internet comes in. I use Rentalhomes.com, the MRIS, and Rentals.com, which has links here and overseas. Stafford is a big military area, so I often lease to people returning from Iraq or Korea. It must be terrifying to consider moving your entire family to an unknown community and residence, but people seem to trust me that much. I thank the Internet for that.

> I HAVE HAD A NUMBER OF MY ADS STOLEN AND REPLICATED ON CRAIGSLIST. SO I'M NOT FOND OF CRAIGSLIST.

**Q:** Do you use Craigslist at all?

**A:** I was a very big supporter of Craigslist in the beginning, but they just don't have the safety features that are required for this industry's privacy issues. Scammers have stolen and replicated my ads for a much lower price, and they're very hard to catch even though I've had the FBI, FTC, CIA and local police involved.

**Q:** Do you do anything with traditional advertising, like newspapers?

**A:** If newspaper listings are linked with the rental websites that I use, I will. For example, what I put on the MRIS automatically goes to the local newspapers.

**Q:** It seems a little bit unusual to have a property management arm of a real estate company. Is that something that is more common in your area, or is it something that was started because there was a customer need?

**A:** It's not common, and there is a huge need. In the private sector, there is really no training or structure for credit applications, background checks, or leases. The average owner or investor can find himself in a "Pacific Heights" situation all too easily. There have been cases where people have moved into a home and destroyed it within days. A management company has excellent training, they draw the best people, and they monitor everything. It's just a completely different environment.

> **THERE HAVE BEEN CASES WHERE PEOPLE HAVE MOVED IN AND WITHIN DAYS, THEY HAVE DESTROYED A HOME.**

**Q:** What do you attribute your success to?
**A:** Listening and really paying attention are the key. Some new managers come into the business thinking tenants have to do what they say and pay their rent, or be thrown out. But it's not that simple, and it's a mistake to have a preconceived notion about a situation. Nine times out of ten, if people are allowed to vent for a while, the real problem or complaint will surface. We're there to balance everything out and try to make the tenant happy. If he leaves, the owner won't be happy.

**Q:** When things don't go particularly well, from where do you draw your strength and inspiration?
**A:** I try to reflect on the things that did go well. You can have a really bad day, with owners and tenants yelling at you; nobody is happy and you just can't seem to win. Then out of the clear blue, a tenant comes in with a cherry pie that she made because you did something nice for her. That makes it all worthwhile. Sounds corny, but it's true.

**Q:** Do you have any slogans that you use?
**A:** "Everything has to be fair." To me, it's very important that everybody has an even and fair playing field.

**Q:** What are some of the biggest challenges you have faced and how have you overcome those challenges?

**A:** The biggest challenges for me in the beginning were construction issues that I couldn't control. For example, I managed an older apartment building which was renovated to include washers and dryers in every unit. Water started flowing back into the apartments and nobody could figure out why. It turned out that the plumbing couldn't handle the new load of water and suds, and all of the tenants were angry about what should have been a big improvement. I had to frantically get on the phone and find a company to fix the problem.

> I ATTRIBUTE MY SUCCESS TO LISTENING.

**Q:** Any tips or tricks that have kept you from repeating the same mistake?

**A:** When you've been through big problems, you don't want to go there again! So I stay open-minded, look at the whole picture, watch for signs of trouble before it happens and pre-empt it.

**Q:** Describe for me your best tenant and also your best owner.

**A:** The best owner listens and gives input, but he lets you do your job because he hired you for your expertise. The best tenant isn't necessarily the one who pays on time or is the cleanest housekeeper, but he follows the rules. He communicates with you if there are problems, so you know what's going on. You only remember 10% of your tenants or clients, because the rest of them do what they are supposed to do.

**Q:** What have been the most rewarding aspects of property management for you?

**A:** It makes you a better person all around: financially, in the way you treat people, and in the way you take care of your own property. There isn't anything that you aren't involved in, it's all encompassing. I like that it's constantly different;

every day is a challenge and a reward.

**Q:** What do you see as some of the biggest opportunities for new property managers coming into the business?

**A:** We need so many more property managers! When I started at Century 21, nobody was really sure about me or the process. Eventually they realized that I really did know the answers, and I was good with people; we were effective and making money. With so many foreclosures and short sales, owners need our help turning their properties into rentals. They may not make their mortgage, but it's a whole lot better than if they had nothing at all. They're not losing the property, and somebody is taking care of it.

*"Success consists of getting up just one more time than you fall."*
-Oliver Goldsmith

*"Personality and organization skills are the most important attributes for an employee."*
James Donnelly, Castle Group

**BACKGROUND**

James Donnelly lives in Weston, Florida. He is the owner, president, and CEO of Castle Group, which is comprised of three corporations: Castle Management, Inc., Castle Guard Security, Inc., and Community Insurance, Inc. Castle Group has 700 employees and manages 200 community associations, 60 of which have an on-site manager.

**INTERVIEW**

Q: How did you get into property management?
A: I grew up in Ottawa, Ontario, Canada. I got my chartered accountant (CA) designation, which is the Canadian equivalent of a CPA. I grew to dislike that industry very quickly, so I started a company that sold real estate investments. We bought apartments in Florida, converted them to condominiums, and then sold them to Canadians. As a result of demand from our absentee investors in these projects, I started a management company. I moved to Florida in 1996 and that's when we launched Castle Group.

Q: Are there any educational classes that you have found to be particularly valuable to you?
A: Getting my CA has been invaluable to me because accounting is a very important function in association management. In Florida you are required to have a community association manager's (CAM) license, and must take continuing education to maintain it. The Community Association Institute

(CAI) provides very good educational products, and is very good at keeping us informed. It's effectively a lobby group on issues that go through the various legislatures.

**Q:** How do you keep up with all the laws that affect your property management business?

**A:** Florida is the most highly-regulated community association state in the country. In our state, many law firms and CPA firms specialize in association management clients. Most of them have a monthly newsletter that keeps us more informed than we even want to be about the laws! We're also required to take a legal update course annually, which is taught by these same attorneys.

**Q:** Are there any books, websites, or other resources that you would recommend?

**A:** CAI has an incredible inventory of books for our industry, two of which are by Peter M. Dunbar, an attorney: *The Law of Florida Homeowners Association* and *The Condominium Concept*. Almost every practitioner in our state would have both of these books on his desk. I'm currently reading *The SPEED of Trust* by Stephen M.R. Covey. He's a very accomplished man and it's one of the best books I've read in a while.

**Q:** How does your company use the Internet to help you with your property management business?

**A:** We have our own website and, even more importantly, the communities now each have a website that we helped design and put in place for them. Owners can go online and make payments, access governing documents, financial statements and board minutes, or put in a request to their board or the company. In high-rise apartments, you can go to the front desk and log in to the guest registry or package tracking system, like an online concierge. For our larger, gated homeowners' association communities, everything is done on the Internet; you can even register a guest visitor and get an e-mail letting you know he has arrived.

**Q:** Do you use any traditional advertising, like newspapers?
**A:** No. We define our market very clearly as A and B properties with full-time on-site managers. There are only 2,000 of those. I can go on the Internet, get a list of directors and addresses from the Florida Department of Corporations, and communicate directly with each one of them. Given this situation, it is inefficient for me to market in a traditional advertising way. However, there are two state community association publications that I see some of my competitors in.

> **WE USE ANTHONY ROBBINS' TERM "CANI!" – CONSTANT AND NEVER-ENDING IMPROVEMENT.**

**Q:** Do you do any PR for your company?
**A:** We just recently hired a PR firm to help us with this. They recommended that I make myself an industry voice, so that it adds credibility to our name and people will look to us as an authority in the industry.

**Q:** What do you attribute your success to?
**A:** We have a constitution that has our defined purpose, vision, values, and a code of conduct. We teach it every day and all employees carry a business card size version of the "Castle Constitution." I always say, "Persistence, persistence, persistence; we might not get it right the first time but we will eventually get it right." We also use Anthony Robbins' term "CANI!" – Constant and Never-ending Improvement. We were an overnight success that took 15 years. We are not the biggest but we believe we are the best and getting better every year.

**Q:** When things don't go particularly well, from where do you draw your strength and inspiration?
**A:** I'm blessed. I married my childhood sweetheart. We've been together 32 years and we have three beautiful children. I just

need to go home and it's all good.

**Q:** Any slogans that you or your company uses?

**A:** Our company tagline is "The Best People, The Best Communities." When you walk into a Ritz Carlton hotel, as soon as you see the lion's head logo, you're expecting a certain guest experience. I attended the Ritz Carlton school called "Legendary Service," where I learned their service practices. Instead of guest experience we call it our resident experience, and it is part of our constant and never-ending improvement process. We're fortunate because our target market is higher end; it's easier to do that and be distinct from our competitors.

**Q:** How do you attract and retain the best employees?

**A:** We create a compelling work environment. We have recently been named one of South Florida's "Best Places to Work." This is not by accident; we've worked very hard at creating the optimal work environment for our team. Last year we invested in a program called "People First" by Jack Lannom. The key theory is that if we can make our team feel important, that's how they'll make our clients feel. We also pay competitively, have a good benefits package, and we are a very fun place to work, with employee appreciation nights, major parties, and raffles for tickets to various concerts and professional sports events. The three owners stand at the front door every Friday night at 5:00 p.m. and thank everybody for their work, so no one leaves this office without an appreciation.

**Q:** What's the most important attribute that you look for in an employee?

**A:** The number one attribute is personality, because of the client engagement. A very close second is organization. This is a business of detail, so if you cannot organize yourself you can't survive.

**Q:** What are you doing now in property management that you wish you had done sooner?

**A:** We tried to serve the entire market for our first ten years. I wish I had figured out more quickly how to focus on the most profitable accounts.

**Q:** What are the biggest mistakes you see new property managers making?

**A:** They get so focused on DOING, that they forget the customer. When a resident enters his high-rise building, he doesn't care what else you're doing. All he knows is the experience he has as he walks through the lobby or comes to the front desk with a request. Property managers forget that the person in front of them is number one.

**Q:** What are some of the biggest challenges that you face?

**A:** Our biggest challenge is growth. When housing starts were so significant during the last ten years, all you had to do was maintain your market share and you had dramatic growth. Now, housing starts have literally gone to zero, so there's no new business coming into the industry. Everyone is competing for the same new accounts and they are everyone's existing ones! To be successful in this situation we have to select, that's our term for hire, the very best talent. We follow a method outlined in a book called *Topgrading* by Bradford Smart. It explains the process we go through to select the best talent.

**Q:** Do you have any tips or tricks that you use to avoid repeating the same mistakes?

**A:** Everything is a process. We need flawless processes and if we have that, then the system can minimize human error. There's always a better way of doing things, and most of our better suggestions come from our clients. We work very, very hard at improving our processes and when we do make a mistake we go back, question the process, and improve it so the problem doesn't happen again.

**Q:** Describe your best client.

**A:** There are three key qualities we like to see in association board members: knowledgeable, decisive, and appreciative. I'd rather have a knowledgeable client because an uninformed one is hard to communicate with or convince. We take direction from the board; they're the decision-making body, so they must be decisive.

**Q:** What is the most rewarding part of the property management business?

**A:** The obvious answer is a happy client, but for me, the most rewarding thing is when I stand out front on Friday night and I say, "Thank you very much for your help this week" to every employee leaving the building. Recently an employee told me, "No, thank you, we couldn't pay our mortgage if we didn't have this job opportunity." We're affecting 700 lives, and I actually get tingles up my spine when I see that everyone on the team has a good life outside the company, which I don't get as much from a client saying "good job." We are in a recession-resistant business, a business that is so unique, so big, and such a huge opportunity for employment.

> **EVERYTHING IS A PROCESS. WE NEED FLAWLESS PROCESSES AND IF WE HAVE THAT, THEN THE SYSTEM CAN MINIMIZE HUMAN ERROR.**

# 32

*"I attribute my success to hard work, listening to people, and having a lot of patience."*
Marc Einhorn, Capitol Management

**BACKGROUND**
Marc Einhorn lives in Bethesda, Maryland. Mark works for Capitol Management as a property manager, with oversight of 15 of the company's 25 commercial properties. Capitol Management was originally established in 1977 under the name The Jaffe Group. They manage office, retail, mixed-use buildings, and some residential units, throughout the Washington D.C. area, Maryland, and Virginia.

**INTERVIEW**
**Q:** How did you get into property management, and did you have a mentor at the time?
**A:** About nine years ago my uncle, Gary Jaffe, owned the company and needed somebody to do property management leasing. At the time, I was between jobs after graduating from college, so I told him, "Absolutely!" He was also my mentor and gave me a lot of guidance.

**Q:** Any educational classes that you have found to be particularly valuable?
**A:** I got my real estate license, and every three years I take 15 hours of continuing education. I also took a couple of classes in property management, and that has been very useful as well.

**Q:** How do you keep up with the various laws that are always changing at the city, state, and federal level?

**A:** You rely on doing your own research, and talking with inspectors and contractors. They should be aware of the latest building codes, and what's expected with tenant build-outs and other types of property development. When you are dealing with architects, they should also be informed on the building codes and the various intricacies that are involved.

> WE GET ABOUT 60% OF LEASING CALLS FROM COSTAR, AND THE OTHER 40% FROM LEASING SIGNS AT THE ACTUAL PROPERTIES.

**Q:** How does your company use the Internet in your property management business?

**A:** We have our own website where we list all of our properties with floor plans, descriptions, and demographics. We also use a company called CoStar, where we put our lease listings, current vacancies, and spaces that might become available down the road. About 60% of my leasing calls come from CoStar, and the other 40% from leasing signs at the actual properties.

**Q:** Do you still do anything in the traditional advertising space, like newspapers?

**A:** I stopped that about five years ago.

**Q:** Do you do any PR for your company?

**A:** Word-of-mouth is our sole source of marketing right now, which I think is the best way to do it.

**Q:** What do you attribute your success to?

**A:** I would attribute my success to hard work, listening to people, taking things in stride, the willingness to put in the time, and having patience. Most property managers don't look at their tenants as "customers," but the tenants are our customers, and we want them to succeed. They are the ones, hopefully, paying the rent and providing the properties with a positive cash flow. I try to trust people in general, treat our tenants with respect, and help them out as much as I can within the terms and stipulations of the lease.

**Q:** When things don't go particularly well and look kind of bleak, from where do you draw your strength and inspiration?

**A:** My parents taught me to work hard and to treat people with respect. You are going to have your good days and your bad days. If things don't work out, you can't dwell on it; you just move on and before you know it, something good is going to come your way.

**Q:** Tell me about the teamwork in your company.

**A:** Our company works as a really good team. We rely on each other's strengths and help out those who are a little weaker in certain areas. My uncle, Gary Jaffe, is such a great man and the one who really motivates all of us. It's a privilege to work with him.

> **MOTIVATION AND INITIATIVE ARE THE MOST IMPORTANT ATTRIBUTES WE LOOK FOR IN AN EMPLOYEE.**

**Q:** How do you attract and retain the best employees?

**A:** We have a great working environment; people really enjoy working here. Everybody gets his work done; we have our holiday parties and take vacations. It's upbeat, we always have a lot going on, and everybody is busy. That's how we keep the train rolling.

**Q:** What is the most important attribute you look for in a new employee?

**A:** Motivation – we look for people who are going to question why we do things a certain way and make suggestions for improvement. We want a "go-getter," someone who has initiative and doesn't just wait to be asked to perform a task.

**Q:** What mistakes do you see new property managers making?

**A:** New property managers need to do a better job at follow-through and show tenants they really care. If a tenant is having a problem with his HVAC or electrical system, they need to make sure it gets taken care of properly. They shouldn't rely on other people, but rather stay on top of things themselves to make sure the customer is satisfied.

**Q:** What are some of the biggest challenges you face and how do you overcome them?
**A:** Collecting rent is a challenge at times, yet it all goes back to treating people with respect and showing them you want them to succeed. If they don't, it can be very difficult to fill the spaces back up. Sometimes you have to give free rent, or reconfigure the space, or put more money into the property. You want them to be motivated to pay you.

**Q:** Do you have any tips or tricks for making sure you avoid repeating the same mistakes?
**A:** Keep good notes and good documentation, such as when working with contractors. We try to get at least three proposals for major projects; you'd be surprised at the variation of the prices that come in for the same job. Learn from all of your experiences and always stay in contact with your tenants. Last, but certainly not least, make sure you don't get discouraged when things go wrong.

> **THE BEST TENANT TAKES CARE OF THE PREMISES, PAYS THE RENT, HAS A LONG-TERM LEASE, AND HAS A GOOD, FINANCIALLY-SOUND BUSINESS.**

**Q:** Describe for me your best tenant.
**A:** The best tenant has a good financial background, a long-term lease, performs the necessary maintenance, and pays the rent before the late fee kicks in. Sometimes we will give nonprofit organizations a below-market rent; it's nice to help them and the community, and perhaps get some good publicity for the company.

**Q:** What has been the most rewarding aspect of doing property management?

**A:** Every day is different, it's never monotonous. I'm not behind a desk, which is great because I really like meeting people and putting deals together. You get the opportunity to learn everything about how to maintain and run buildings, the different types of leases, working with people and contractors. There is a lot involved, and you can take everything you learn back to your own personal life as well.

*"Success seems to be connected with action. Successful people keep moving. They make mistakes, but they don't quit."*
-Conrad Hilton

# 33

*"This is where a lot of our presidents come, so we've learned to deal with the Secret Service as well."*
Stephen Francis, Pristine Property Management of Martha's Vineyard

## BACKGROUND
Stephen Francis lives in Vineyard Haven, Massachusetts. He has been in the property management business for 27 years and is an owner and operator of Pristine Property Management of Martha's Vineyard. The company currently has six employees and 18 clients. Stephen manages 15 multi-million dollar vacation properties and four commercial properties.

## INTERVIEW
**Q:** How did you get into property management?
**A:** It was purely by accident. My wife and I had gotten burnt out on our jobs, and answered an ad for caretakers for a property. It was very tough, but that learning experience catapulted us into the field and got us moving on to bigger and better things.

**Q:** Were there any educational classes you took along the way that you found particularly valuable?
**A:** I'm self-taught, and it was trial and error for the first few years. I've always been mechanically inclined and in off times would get certified in a new field, like pool maintenance. If there was a maintenance problem that I didn't know all the specific details about, I would find someone in that field and learn from him.

**Q:** How do you keep up with all the laws that affect your property management business?

**A:** I have to keep up with all the local laws because they constantly change and are determined by each town's bylaws. For instance, a vacation rental can't be shared by two families unless they are related. We even learned to deal with the Secret Service because a lot of our presidents spend their vacations here. Our restrictions and laws aren't normal compared to the rest of the country!

**Q:** Do you belong to any professional associations?
**A:** We just belong to a couple of the nonprofit clubs, where most of the trades people get together and pick each other's brains, relax, and have a beer. We represent a number of businesses: solar, major construction, renovations, plumbing, electrical. You name it, we're all here.

**Q:** How do you use the Internet and other technology tools to help you with your property management business?
**A:** We have our own website and I've been dabbling with Facebook and Twitter, which has helped to get our name out there. A few of our properties are smart houses and, nine times out of 10, via phone or computer, I can rectify problems with the home's audiovisual system, turn off the alarms, adjust the heat, turn on the sprinklers, and control the lighting.

> **YOU CAN'T HAVE TWO DIFFERENT FAMILIES RENTING ONE PROPERTY UNLESS THEY ARE ALL PART OF ONE EXTENDED FAMILY.**

**Q:** Do you use any traditional advertising, like newspapers?
**A:** For the last 27 years we have gotten most of our business through referrals.

**Q:** What do you attribute your success to?
**A:** In this field, you have to understand your properties and the area they're in. Martha's Vineyard is a different world, an island; we have to deal with the humidity, the winds, the

weather itself, with conservation committees. There are a lot of ecological issues that we have to watch out for. You can't just go and cut down a tree in the backyard because it's blocking your satellite dish. Everything requires a permit, and the town fathers will let you know if you can do it or not.

**Q:** Are there any slogans that your company uses?
**A:** We are a green company. Everything is recycled, and all of our cleaning and landscaping is done with organic or homemade supplies, no pesticides. You have to be careful here because substances can leach into the drinking water sources. Local restrictions are placing an emphasis on natural and organic approaches now, but it's been tough on some of the smaller companies because the materials are more expensive.

**Q:** How do you attract and retain the best employees?
**A:** We're an island, so that's pretty simple: we all know each other. It's easy to learn who is actually qualified to do the work, and how good they are. If you mess up, the whole island will know about it in a day or two! I hand pick my employees, relying on people that I personally know and have done business with in the past.

**Q:** What are the most important attributes you look for in an employee?
**A:** They have to be responsible, dependable, and knowledgeable, which is difficult to find here on the island. A lot of the people we hire come from off-island and take a ferry here every day. When you find people you can count on you don't want to lose them, so we have to take a bit of a hit and pay them a lot more than what they'd make off-island. But, in the long run it keeps everything running smoothly and the properties well maintained, which gets us the referrals that we need in order to grow.

> **WE ARE A GREEN COMPANY. EVERYTHING IS RECYCLED AND ORGANIC.**

**Q:** What are the biggest mistakes that you see new property managers making?

**A:** They don't familiarize themselves with their properties enough. You have to have a preventative maintenance program in place and use it on a daily basis, because things can start deteriorating fast.

**Q:** What are some of the biggest challenges that you are facing?

**A:** One challenge is being familiar with the individual properties, because each one has its own problems. Oceanfront properties are maintained in a totally different way than inner island properties, for example, because of the shore and the coastline. My biggest challenge is keeping up with new laws, regulations and environmental issues, especially when the federal, state, and county governments all want to be in charge and tell us what to do.

**Q:** Describe for me your best client.

**A:** Our best clients understand that we know what we are doing, that this is not New York City and we live by a whole different set of rules out here. They trust us to maintain their properties to the utmost peak of performance, and save them money. With my clients, I put a cap of $1,000 on any repairs or purchases before taking bids, and I only deal with contractors or vendors that I personally know and can depend on. We haven't raised any of our prices in seven years.

> I LOOK FOR EMPLOYEES WHO ARE RESPONSIBLE, DEPENDABLE, AND KNOWLEDGEABLE, WHICH IS DIFFICULT TO FIND HERE ON THE ISLAND.

**Q:** What has been the most rewarding aspect of property management for you?

**A:** I'm in control of what I'm doing and I enjoy it. That makes it a lot easier. If you don't know what you're doing or enjoy it, then it just becomes your job and tends to wear you down.

**Q:** What do you see as some of the biggest opportunities for property managers getting into the business?

**A:** There is a lot of opportunity for someone who's interested in the caretaking field. My friend Gary Dunn puts out a paper called *The Caretaker Gazette*, which lists all kinds of maintenance, property management, and caretaking positions worldwide. A lot of people need these services, and either pay a salary or trade labor for a place to live. But I can't stress it enough: it's all about preventative maintenance, and you have to be up on what you are doing to make it in this field.

> **MY BIGGEST CHALLENGE IS KEEPING UP WITH ALL THE NEW LAWS, REGULATIONS, AND ENVIRONMENTAL ISSUES.**

*"Success is how high you bounce when you hit bottom."*

-George S. Patton

*"People skills are critical because we are in a people business."*
Vickie Gaskill, Bell Anderson Associates, LLC

**BACKGROUND**

Vickie Gaskill lives in Kent, Washington. She is a co-owner and designated broker of Bell Anderson Associates, LLC. The company was established in 1963 and currently has 18 employees. They manage about 40 community associations (almost 3,000 units), 225 single-family homes, and approximately 120 apartment units. Vickie has been a member of the National Association of Residential Property Managers (NARPM) since 1994, a board member for three years, and will be its national president in 2010.

**INTERVIEW**

Q: How did you get into property management?
A: I was looking for something to do after my husband and I sold our carpet cleaning business. I first joined Bell Anderson to balance some old accounts and act as bookkeeper. Within a year I got my real estate license and took a property management position with the company. I bought Bell Anderson in 2002, and the rest is history.

Q: Are there any educational classes that you have taken that have been particularly valuable?
A: The trade associations offer designation classes that are paramount to getting an education, and I have four designations pertinent to my career. The college classes I took in speech, accounting, and human resources were also very valuable.

**Q:** How do you keep up with all the laws that affect your property management business?

**A:** The best way is being involved in one of the trade associations, because every single one of them has some kind of legislative arm. In particular, there are the National Association of Residential Property Managers (NARPM) and the National Association of Realtors (NAR).

**Q:** Any books that you have read that you have found to be particularly valuable to you?

**A:** The Institute of Real Estate Management (IREM) and the National Apartment Association (NAA) have courses and books on all kinds of property management: shopping centers, high-rise office buildings, single-family homes, apartment buildings; I was privileged to co-author a book on community association management for IREM. These trade associations are helping colleges write courses for property management degree programs. I also co-authored a course on community associations for North Seattle Community College.

> I ATTRIBUTE MY SUCCESS TO A LOT OF HARD WORK AND A VERY SUPPORTIVE FAMILY.

**Q:** What kind of PR are you doing for your company?

**A:** I've done interviews like crazy; for instance, I was invited to speak about community association management on a local real estate talk show. I'm also very involved in the community so that the Bell Anderson name is out there. Our company won first place in a recycling competition, and the event was covered by three local TV networks and the *Seattle Times*. You can't pay for that kind of publicity.

**Q:** What do you attribute your success to?

**A:** It's due to a lot of hard work, and wonderful family support, too. My daughters and nieces work here, and my husband of 40 years has been very supportive.

**Q:** When things don't go particularly well, from where do you draw your strength and inspiration?

**A:** I have a "Feel Good Book" filled with my collection of awards, notes of thanks, funny jokes, even autographs and photos from sports figures; I'm kind of a sports freak. When things get rough that book really does help me.

**Q:** Are there any slogans you use personally or that the company uses?

**A:** Our company tagline is "Our family, serving your family," probably because we have so many family members here, and we work in that type of environment. I also like the quote from Tim Russert's father, "Always blessed, but never entitled."

> **IN OUR HIRING PROCESS WE NOW DO PERSONALITY PROFILING.**

**Q:** How do you attract and retain the best employees?

**A:** We treat our employees with dignity and respect, and make them happy. I probably now have the best working crew I've ever had at Bell Anderson, and would hate to lose any one of them. They have good abilities and attitudes and have melded as a team.

**Q:** What is the most important attribute you look for in an employee?

**A:** The number one thing I look for is people skills: how they interact with others, their eye contact and body language. People skills are critical because we are in a people business. My favorite interview question is, "Tell me about a difficult client you've had, or a difficult situation you have encountered."

**Q:** What are you doing now in your business that you wish you had done sooner?

**A:** We now do personality profiling in our hiring process, and we've found some good people that way. That's one thing I wish I had done a lot sooner.

**Q:** What are some of the biggest mistakes you see new property managers making?
**A:** They are very impatient and don't take the time to cultivate their client relationships; they want everything now or want it "yesterday." Instead they should be taking some time to work with their owners and help them see something a different way.

**Q:** What are some of the biggest challenges you face and how have you overcome those challenges?
**A:** The economy means we've had to make some challenging spending decisions. I've always been open and honest with our employees, sharing the company's financial information and business results with them, so that they know when and why things are a little tight.

**Q:** Any tips or tricks you use to avoid repeating the same mistake?
**A:** We do book studies as a group. A couple of years back, I realized we needed to work on our attitudes a little bit. I found a book, *Delivering Knock Your Socks Off Service* by Kristin Anderson and Ron Zemke. We did a three-month book study on it, which included book reports at staff meetings. It seems to stick in your head better when you have that kind of participation, and you have a better buy-in from the employee.

> **THE BIGGEST MISTAKE NEW PROPERTY MANAGERS MAKE IS THAT THEY DON'T TAKE THE TIME TO CULTIVATE THEIR CLIENT RELATIONSHIPS.**

**Q:** Describe for me your best client, your best tenant, and your best board member.
**A:** My best client appreciates my knowledge, works with me,

and teaches me something. My best tenant takes care of the unit and pays the rent on time. And my best board members behave like board members; they remove all of their personal agendas, treat us with respect, and work at good decision-making. Ideally they've also served in some type of leadership or volunteer role before, and they understand how a board works.

**Q:** What is the most rewarding aspect of the property management business?

**A:** It's never dull. I would never have met the people I know, across the nation, if I weren't involved in this profession. I'm a people person, and I enjoy that aspect a lot. I've received so much good information, not only for my business, but to make myself even better, too.

**Q:** What are some of the biggest opportunities you see for new property managers?

**A:** Every product being built today has some sort of association arrangement, and rentals will always be around because not everyone can buy real estate. There are lots of opportunities for new property managers; if you want to get into this field, I don't know how you could go wrong!

> **MY BEST CLIENT IS SOMEONE WHO APPRECIATES MY KNOWLEDGE, WHO WORKS WITH ME TO MAKE GOOD DECISIONS, AND WHO TEACHES ME SOMETHING.**

*"The only place where success comes before work is in the dictionary."*
                                    *-Vidal Sassoon*

# 35

*"Creating great places to live, and work, and shop."*
Samuel Goldstein, Galman Group

**BACKGROUND**

Samuel Goldstein works in Jenkintown, Pennsylvania. Samuel has been with the Galman Group since 1988 and is currently Chief Financial Officer. The company was established in 1991 and has 170 employees. They manage 27 apartment developments (4,400 units), 14 condominium developments (1,900 units), and one office building.

**INTERVIEW**

**Q:** How did you get into property management?
**A:** I am a CPA, and I was working at a CPA firm when I got the opportunity to work for the Galman Group. I've been here ever since.

**Q:** Any educational classes that you have found to be particularly valuable?
**A:** I got a masters degree in real estate from New York University after working in the field for 15 years. It was a pretty interesting and worthwhile experience, because I found that it validated some of the things that we did, and invalidated some things too.

**Q:** How do you keep up with all the laws that affect your property management business?
**A:** In Pennsylvania you're required to have extensive continuing education every year to keep your CPA certification current. With regard to property management, the National Apart-

ment Association (NAA) plays an integral part in keeping on top of changes in the laws. I also rely on the Apartment Association of Greater Philadelphia, the NAA magazine called *Units*, and a monthly newsletter called *Property Management Monthly*.

Q: Any books that you would recommend?
A: *The Tipping Point* by Malcolm Gladwell, and *The Accidental Billionaires* by Ben Mezrich.

Q: How does your company use the Internet to help you with your property management business?
A: We use the Internet for ordering supplies and processing work orders. Our tenants use it to find us, to do rental applications, and to make rent payments.

Q: Does the company use any of the social media tools like Facebook, Twitter, or LinkedIn?
A: Yes, we use Facebook for one of our marketing tools, with a page set up for two of our locations that have a fairly young demographic.

Q: What about traditional advertising, do you still use newspapers?
A: We've weaned ourselves from print newspapers, although we'll still periodically jump in for a weekend edition when needed, or advertise in the Apartment Guide. Our number one resource is curb appeal; 70-80% of our tenants come from resident referrals. The other 20-30% comes from advertising, which is almost exclusively on the Internet. We've improved our website, done some paid search engine optimization, we use Craigslist, and we recently started using the Call Source service. This allows us to

> **WE HAVE A FACEBOOK PAGE SET UP FOR TWO OF OUR LOCATIONS BECAUSE THE RESIDENTS THERE ARE A FAIRLY YOUNG DEMOGRAPHIC.**

track the source of our calls because each ad has a specific ID number and phone number.

**Q:** Do you do any PR for your company?
**A:** We have a PR person and we do PR when we have grand openings or big development projects. The current economic environment made us aware of the need to more aggressively market the company name.

**Q:** What do you attribute your success to?
**A:** On a personal level, I'm a big believer in hard work and staying involved. On a company level, we believe in on-site property management, having people on the grounds. Our philosophy has always been: keep the assets in good shape, don't defer improvements even at the expense of cash flow if necessary, and have good people – you have to have good people to be successful.

> **EACH AD HAS A SPECIFIC ID NUMBER AND PHONE NUMBER SO WE CAN TRACK THE SOURCE OF OUR CALLS.**

**Q:** When things don't go particularly well, from where do you draw your strength and inspiration?
**A:** I draw on my family and my friends.

**Q:** Any slogans that you use personally or that the company uses?
**A:** Our company founder's slogan is "Creating great places to live, and work, and shop." We have monthly speakers or trips, and continental breakfasts. Once or twice a year, around the holidays, we host a party for residents which our employees and families attend too.

**Q:** How do you attract and retain the best employees?
**A:** We have a good reputation, a good corporate culture, competitive pay, and we treat everyone respectfully, with a "small company" atmosphere. We promote from within whenev-

er possible, and invest in our employees through training. We've had very little turnover.

Q: What's the most important attribute that you look for in an employee?
A: The most important thing to look for is a good work ethic.

Q: What are you doing now in the company that you wish you had started doing sooner?
A: Education and training are so important, and I'd have emphasized that more. If we're going to continually promote people to higher levels of responsibility, we need to give them the necessary training. One way we've done that is by plugging into various educational outlets through a number of the associations that we belong to. Drexel University recently partnered with the local apartment association to offer a property management degree program. People can now make this a real profession, which is a good thing.

> WE INVEST IN OUR EMPLOYEES THROUGH TRAINING. WE HAVE HAD VERY LITTLE TURNOVER.

Q: What are the biggest mistakes you see new property managers making?
A: Being sloppy and not paying attention to details are big mistakes. They lead to things like failure to get proper approvals, choosing vendors without first getting bids, and paying a vendor invoice when they did inferior work. Some managers also stay behind their desks too much and don't get out and about to their properties.

Q: What are some of the biggest challenges that you are facing?
A: Budgeting and refinancing for the next few years will be a big challenge, because asset values have changed so much and will continue to change.

**Q:** What have been the most rewarding aspects of your property management business?

**A:** We regularly survey our residents and ask them to rate our performance in a number of areas. It's very rewarding when we get nice comments on how we're doing, or a complimentary phone call about an employee.

**Q:** What are some of the biggest opportunities you see for new property managers?

**A:** There are some real opportunities in property management and homeowners associations, and a well-rounded person can enter those fields and have relatively rapid growth. Many of the responsibilities are identical, although the fees for a homeowners association are small compared to managing an apartment community. And it's very tough, a job that not many people want to do. They have to be hardworking and aggressive, but they can make a pretty good living.

> **THERE ARE SOME REAL OPPORTUNITIES IN PROPERTY MANAGEMENT ON THE CONDOMINIUM AND HOMEOWNERS ASSOCIATION SIDE.**

*"There is no success without hardship."*
                              -Sophocles

# 36

*"Don't sweat the small stuff, and at the end of the day, everything is the small stuff."*
Philip Henderson, Henderson Properties, Inc.

**BACKGROUND**

Philip Henderson lives in Charlotte, North Carolina and is the president of Henderson Properties, which was established in 1998 and presently has 34 employees. The company manages 370 rental properties (single-family, town homes, condominiums, small apartment buildings, offices), and 73 community associations.

**INTERVIEW**

**Q:** How did you get into property management?

**A:** I got my real estate broker's license in 1990 and started investing in properties. A friend of mine asked me to help him buy his first house, then to manage it as a rental when he got transferred. Shortly after that he referred another owner to me, and from there it just snowballed. Before long I was managing 50 properties for other people, in addition to 20 or so properties of my own.

**Q:** What educational classes have you taken that you have found to be particularly valuable?

**A:** I have taken a lot of classes through the Charlotte Realtor's Association and the National Association of Residential Property Managers (NARPM). I've attended some of NARPM's national conventions and those have been a great help to me as well.

**Q:** How do you keep up with all the laws that affect your property management business?

A: NARPM does a great job of constantly updating us on the current trends and changes in laws.

Q: Are there any books that you would recommend?

A: *Landlording* by Leigh Robinson and *Managing Rental Properties for Maximum Profit* by Greg Perry.

Q: Any other useful resources that you would recommend?

A: For association management I highly recommend the Community Associations Institute (CAIonline.org), which is very similar to NARPM. It's a great resource for community association managers and board members to find help with board-related problems, policies and procedures.

Q: How do you use the Internet to help you with your property management business?

A: We have our own website, HendersonProperties.com, where we list all of our available rentals and information about our rental and association management services. We utilize a search engine optimization (SEO) company to ensure that we're one of the first results when people are searching for services like ours.

Q: Do you use any social media tools like Facebook, Twitter, or LinkedIn?

A: We currently have a Facebook page, and we're in the process of getting on LinkedIn and Twitter as well. Our marketing firm handles all of our company advertising, including the weekly updates on these sites. We also have a blog on our website that shares company news like our current events, a new contract, or a new community association.

> FOR COMMUNITY ASSOCIATION MANAGEMENT I HIGHLY RECOMMEND THE COMMUNITY ASSOCIATIONS INSTITUTE (CAI). THEIR WEBSITE IS CAIONLINE.ORG.

**Q:** Do you do anything with traditional advertising, like newspapers?
**A:** No, we stopped classified ads over two years ago because we just weren't getting any results. Now we advertise solely on the Internet, on 15 to 20 different websites.

**Q:** Do you do any PR for your company?
**A:** Our marketing firm handles all of our PR, which is more for building brand awareness than for rentals or services. We've used kiosks in local shopping malls, online banner ads for the local newspaper's website, and direct mail pieces to investors, touting our property management services.

> WE CURRENTLY HAVE A FACEBOOK PAGE FOR OUR COMPANY, AND WE ARE IN THE PROCESS OF CREATING A LINKEDIN PAGE AND SETTING UP TWITTER AS WELL.

**Q:** What do you attribute your success to?
**A:** One reason for our success is that Charlotte experienced a very rapid growth in the recent past, increasing the need for management of rental properties and new community associations. The second reason is that we find and keep good quality employees – this has really been the key to growing our business and keeping our current customer base happy.

**Q:** Do you have any particular slogans that you use?
**A:** "Don't sweat the small stuff, and at the end of the day, everything is the small stuff."

**Q:** How do you attract and retain the best employees?
**A:** We attract good employees because they see the friendly, family atmosphere that is our company culture. We're a stable company that offers potential for advancement, with an open environment that encourages input from all employ-

ees. We recognize people's achievements at staff meetings on a regular basis and hold holiday parties and other activities that encourage a sense of teamwork. Our employees know that their opinions matter, and that they will be rewarded for a job well done.

Q: What do you see as the most important attribute to look for in a new employee?
A: I need to know I can trust an employee to be truthful with me and do the best job he possibly can. I don't micromanage; the last thing I want to do is look over somebody's shoulder every day to make sure he's doing what he's supposed to be doing.

Q: What are you doing now in property management that you feel like you should have done sooner?
A: I should have revamped our website, search engine optimization, and online marketing a lot sooner than I did. I also should have hired department managers to supervise various employees, instead of trying to do it all myself.

Q: What do you see as the biggest mistakes that new property managers are making?
A: Some realtors and others jumping into the property management business think it is so easy, but they don't really know what they are doing. They haven't had any training or education, or joined associations like NARPM, or done any research. Their mistakes make the rest of the industry look bad.

> WE ARE ABLE TO ATTRACT GOOD EMPLOYEES BECAUSE OF OUR COMPANY CULTURE.

Q: What are some of the biggest challenges that you face and how do you overcome those challenges?
A: We're competing with new property management companies who provide a very basic level of service and charge

accordingly. We have to convince investors that our slightly higher management fees mean they will receive the expertise and service that will be more profitable for them in the long run; their properties will be rented faster, to better tenants. Just getting properties rented is a challenge in an economic slowdown because of the decrease in demand and the increase in supply.

> **WHEN HIRING SOMEONE, I TRY TO DETERMINE IF I CAN TRUST THAT EMPLOYEE TO BE TRUTHFUL WITH ME AND DO THE BEST JOB HE POSSIBLY CAN.**

**Q:** Any tips or tricks that help you in some way avoid repeating the same mistakes?

**A:** We have written processes and procedures for everything we do, and we'll make changes to them if necessary, upon review. We always try and learn from our mistakes.

**Q:** Describe your best tenant and your best client.

**A:** Our best tenant pays his rent on time, contacts us with maintenance issues, and is a considerate neighbor who keeps the property up and the noise level down. Our best client (investor) trusts us and allows us to do our job.

**Q:** What have been the most rewarding aspects of your property management business?

**A:** We enjoy helping people find a place to live and to make that place as comfortable as possible. From a client standpoint, we enjoy helping investors to achieve the financial goals they have for their investment properties.

**Q:** What do you see as some of the biggest opportunities for new property managers?

**A:** My advice for any new property managers getting into the business would be to join an established firm with a good training program. They'll learn the correct way to manage community associations or rental properties.

*"Success is to be measured not so much by the position that one has reached in life as by the obstacles which he has overcome."*
-Booker T. Washington

# 37

*"The happier you are, the more money you make."*
Trevor Henson, First Light Property Management, Inc.

**BACKGROUND**
Trevor Henson lives in Manhattan Beach, California, and has been in the real estate industry for six years. Trevor is one of three partners with First Light Property Management, Inc., which was established in 2006. The company manages 15 multi-family properties comprised of 16 to 54 units each.

**INTERVIEW**
Q: How did you get into property management?
A: I was a project manager for some hotel construction in Costa Rica in 2006, and then I became an on-site manager for one hotel while another was being renovated. Soon, local residents were asking me to look after and rent out their homes or condos while they were out of the country, and that was my start in property management.

Q: Any educational classes that you have taken that you have found to be particularly valuable?
A: I took a project/construction management course at UCLA through their continuing education program, and I got my B.S. in business administration and information systems from the Marshall School of Business at the University of Southern California (USC).

Q: How do you keep up with all the new laws that affect your property management business?
A: The Apartment Owners' Association (AOA) has seminars,

trade shows, and a monthly magazine that's helpful. We're very up to speed on the various local and national blogs as well. One of the best blogs for multi-family industry information is MultiFamilyInsiders.com. They cover topics like the current market, property management strategies, and different laws. We post our blog there and we're pretty active on it.

> ONE OF THE BIGGEST AND BEST BLOGS THAT WE USE IS MULTIFAMILYINSIDERS.COM.

**Q:** Any recommended books that you have found to be particularly valuable?

**A:** *California Real Estate Property Management* by Fred Crane, *The Seven Secrets to Successful Apartment Leasing* by Eric Cumley, and *Property Management* by Robert C. Kyle.

**Q:** Any websites or other educational resources that you would recommend?

**A:** First, I would recommend MultiFamilyInsiders.com. That is a great resource. Also, Mike Brewer's property management blog, www.mbrewergroup.com, and Lisa Trosien's apartment marketing blog, www.apartmentmarketingblog.com. They're both great resources for apartment industry information and discussion.

**Q:** How do you use the Internet to help you with your property management business?

**A:** We've used social media tools extensively since 2009, which have increased our web traffic significantly. We have over 1,000 "followers" and growing on Twitter, a blog, a LinkedIn site, a Facebook fan page, and we are currently working on our Squidoo lens. We do search engine optimization (SEO) for our website, and we have multiple listings on Yahoo Local and Google Local. We even accept rental applications and rent payments on our website.

**Q:** So what do you actually tweet on Twitter?
**A:** I've set up a view in Netvibes which pulls in numerous RSS feeds from Google, Technorati, Blogger, MultiFamilyInsiders.com, and others. I search for different keywords such as "property management" or "multi-family renters." I check this every day or so, and when I find some interesting and useful news I put it out over Twitter. My company logo is next to the Tweet with a link back to my website; I usually get an additional three to four followers a day.

> WE USE SOCIAL MEDIA TOOLS EXTENSIVELY. I SPEND ABOUT EIGHT TO 10 HOURS A WEEK ON IT.

**Q:** How much time do you spend on a weekly basis in the social media arena?
**A:** About eight to 10 hours a week.

**Q:** Do you do any traditional advertising?
**A:** We do some direct mail campaigns with 4x6 postcards, and marketing calls to owner prospects, but we don't do any newspaper advertising. All of our vacancies are advertised through various Internet listing services and on our company web page.

**Q:** What do you attribute your success to?
**A:** I'd say my education from the business school at USC, and having a strong network of educated and reliable contacts.

**Q:** Any slogans that you use personally or your company uses?
**A:** "The happier you are, the more money you make."

**Q:** How do you attract and retain the best employees?
**A:** I use Craigslist exclusively to advertise for my employees. We offer pretty standard benefits and keep a positive, entrepreneurial atmosphere in which to work. We'll sit around and

brainstorm as a company and elicit ideas, feedback, and suggestions. Every employee's ideas are considered.

**Q:** What's the most important attribute you look for in an employee?
**A:** You have to have drive, and be able to think "outside the box." Our company is built on that.

**Q:** What are you doing now in your property management business that you feel you should have been doing sooner?
**A:** I wish I had started participating in various networking groups a lot sooner, like the local Chamber of Commerce and Business Network International (BNI), because it's done nothing but help our business. We've gotten some great contacts like good quality electricians, plumbers, and realtors through them.

> DRIVE AND "OUT OF THE BOX" THINKING ARE THE MOST IMPORTANT ATTRIBUTES FOR AN EMPLOYEE.

**Q:** What are the biggest mistakes that you see new property managers making?
**A:** The way we reach and service our clients and tenants is changing. New property managers shouldn't run their business the exact same way as it's been done for the last 30 years. They need to embrace technology while still keeping the human touch required in our industry.

**Q:** What are some of the biggest challenges that you face, and how do you overcome those challenges?
**A:** The recession is causing high vacancy rates, so we've started doing some really aggressive marketing. The most effective tactic we've found is getting back to people within half an hour of contact, whether it's by e-mail or phone. They're looking at 10 other rentals at the same time, and the first person to get back to them will be the one uppermost in their minds.

**Q:** Any tips or tricks to help avoid repeating the same mistakes?

**A:** We have monthly meetings and take minutes to cover what goals were accomplished in the previous month, what went right and what went wrong. I also keep a handwritten journal so when history inevitably repeats itself, I can go back and take a look at how I dealt with a similar situation.

**Q:** Describe your best client.

**A:** Our best client is someone who has a good job and education. He doesn't constantly look over our shoulder, and nickel-and-dime everything we do; he just wants updates and sound information from us. He trusts us to do our job.

**Q:** Describe your best tenant.

**A:** Our best tenant pays his rent and keeps the place up. He updates us with building concerns, like a leaky pipe under a sink, and helps to keep little problems from potentially turning into large ones.

**Q:** What is the most rewarding aspect of your property management business?

**A:** The most rewarding aspect is getting involved in the owner's dream for his property. We will sit down and figure out where he plans to go with it: sell it or convert it later, pass it on to his kids? Once we know that, together we can come up with a strategy for managing the property. When an owner eventually realizes the goal or dream, it's fulfilling for us because we helped facilitate it, and we usually become really good friends in the process. It's more of a joint project than it is us providing a service.

> **THE MOST REWARDING ASPECT OF OUR PROPERTY MANAGEMENT BUSINESS IS GETTING INVOLVED IN THE OWNER'S DREAM FOR HIS PROPERTY.**

**Q:** What do you see as some of the biggest opportunities for new property managers?

**A:** There are so many new technologies coming out all the time. New property managers need to find and capitalize on the ones that will make them more efficient, reduce overhead, and give them ways to provide their clients with new services.

---

**Author's Note:**
Be sure to check out *Appendix E* for Trevor Henson's ***Online Marketing and Social Media for Property Management***

---

# 38

*"I look for employees who are honest and ethical."*
Charlie Koons, Mountain-n-Plains Real Estate Services, Inc.

**BACKGROUND**
Charlie Koons lives in Fort Collins, Colorado. Charlie founded Mountain-n-Plains Property Management (now Mountain-n-Plains Real Estate Services) in 1979. Currently the company has 19 employees and over 300 clients. They manage 518 residential houses, apartments, and condos, and five million square feet of commercial property.

**INTERVIEW**
**Q:** How did you get into property management?
**A:** I bought my first investment house with a friend of mine, and I did all the showings after my regular job, along with the painting and repairs. By 1976 we had four units, then decided to sell all of them to a woman who said she'd pay full price if I managed them for her. That's when I became a property manager. My friend and I made up the name Mountain-n-Plains because both of us came from Kansas and we had moved to the mountains.

**Q:** When you got into property management did you have a mentor?
**A:** Not initially, but after the first couple of years Dean Whiteman, CPM, became my mentor. He got me involved with the professional property management organizations and the Fort Collins Board of Realtors. He encouraged me to further my education in the field and to make it a professional career.

**Q:** Any educational classes you have taken that have proven to be particularly valuable to you?

**A:** The most valuable educational classes have been the ones I've taken from the Institute of Real Estate Management (IREM). They're very intensive programs, and you have to write a management thesis at the end. By taking those courses you can get your Certified Property Management (CPM) and your Accredited Management Organization (AMO) designations.

**Q:** How do you keep up with all the new laws that affect property management?

**A:** If you have a Colorado real estate license you have to take the mandatory update course every year. You constantly need to attend various courses, trade shows, and professional organization events, and keep talking to other property managers.

**Q:** Are there any books or periodicals that you have found particularly useful?

**A:** Two good monthly periodicals are the *UNITS* magazine from the National Apartment Association (NAA), and the *Journal of Property Management* (JPM) from IREM. I don't care how many books you read, though; until you have some real-life, practical property management experience, you'll never really know if this profession is for you.

**Q:** Are there other associations that you also belong to?

**A:** We belong to the Board of Realtors, the Commercial Board of Realtors, the local Chamber of Commerce, the Better Business Bureau, the Apartment Association, the National Association of Residential Property Managers (NARPM), IREM, and the Everett Real Estate School at

> **TWO GOOD MONTHLY PERIODICALS ARE THE *UNITS* MAGAZINE FROM NAA AND THE *JOURNAL OF PROPERTY MANAGEMENT* FROM IREM.**

Colorado State University (CSU). Also, we belong to a group of property managers from the Northwest part of the United States; no one is in anyone else's market area.

> **IT REALLY HELPS TO HAVE A SENSE OF HUMOR IN THIS BUSINESS.**

We meet three times a year and we bounce things off of each other all the time: better ways of doing business, computer tips and advice, employee productivity and morale, all kinds of things. It's been very beneficial.

**Q:** How do you use the Internet to help you with your property management business?

**A:** We get our most productive leads from the Internet. Of course we have our own website, but others, such as NorthernColoradoRentals.com, reach a more diverse client base.

**Q:** Does your company use any of the social media tools like Twitter, LinkedIn, or Facebook?

**A:** Our website had a link to Twitter, but we didn't find it to be terribly productive. It is still in its infancy as far as property management is concerned.

**Q:** What do you do for your company's PR?

**A:** We treat our employees and clients well, make them happy, keep the properties rented and well maintained. They'll promote our company for us by word of mouth.

**Q:** What do you attribute your success to?

**A:** You're selling a couple of things in property management: integrity and honesty. Do it every day and you will be a success.

**Q:** When things get a little bleak, from where do you draw your strength and inspiration?

**A:** It really helps to have a sense of humor in this business.

**Q:** What type of person will make the best property manager?
**A:** You have to have a sense of humor and be an incredible Jack or Jill of All Trades, multi-task all the time and like it. There are some people who want to start and finish a task, and don't want to be interrupted while they do. This is not the business for them. I have a bookkeeping job for you if you like a black-and-white type of job. Property management is in the gray area a lot of the time.

> **THE BEST PROPERTY MANAGER IS SOMEONE WHO IS ABLE TO MULTI-TASK ALL THE TIME AND LIKES IT.**

**Q:** Do you have any slogans that you personally use or that your company uses?
**A:** One of our former employees came up with a slogan that we only tell to other property managers or people in the trade: "You can stay home and stick pins in your eyes or you can do property management – it's about the same pain level." Some others are: "If it was easy everybody would be doing it," and "It's not a problem, it's a challenge."

**Q:** How do you attract and retain the best employees?
**A:** You pay as well as you can, better than the rest of the industry in your area – and you really stand behind your employees' decisions. We have a good business reputation and we provide a comfortable place to work.

**Q:** What do you think are the most important attributes to look for in an employee?
**A:** Employees have to be ethical and honest. They won't be afraid to admit to a client that they made a mistake, look him in the eye and apologize, and make it right.

**Q:** What are the biggest mistakes you see new property managers making?
**A:** All new property managers say they'll go the extra mile, but very few of them do and there's no follow-through on their

word. Typically young property managers don't have a one-year business plan, let alone a five-year plan, which is essential.

Some grow too fast. Some aren't accessible enough to their clients. If you don't want to take calls from seven in the morning till seven in the evening, and sometimes on the weekends, you'd better choose a different line of work.

**Q:** What are some of the biggest challenges that you face?
**A:** The biggest challenge is communicating. We all just whip off e-mails to each other, but none of us sit face to face and talk to each other any more. We don't use the phone very much either.

**Q:** How would you contrast residential property management with commercial property management? You've got a lot of experience in both.
**A:** Residential management is the toughest property management you'll ever do, the biggest challenge you'd have in your career. You have to know what you're doing and be the ultimate problem solver, because you'll have 500 houses with their own kind of stove, sets of steps, etc. Keeping the property maintained is the tenants' responsibility, but they're not going to mow the lawn if they don't want to. Commercial property management is easier in many ways, like tenant contact, but you have to be much more sophisticated about budgets, spreadsheets, forecasts, triple net charges, billing tenants back, attracting tenants, and keeping tenants.

> **THE BIGGEST MISTAKE NEW PROPERTY MANAGERS MAKE IS NOT FOLLOWING THROUGH ON THEIR WORD.**

**Q:** Do you have any funny or bizarre stories relative to your property management business?

**A:** I had a resident once who had a miniature pony as a service animal, in a second-story apartment with hardwood floors and concrete steps up to the landing!

**Q:** What is the most rewarding aspect of your property management business?

**A:** It's very rewarding to be known in your community as the "property solver guru." I really enjoy it when people come to me for advice on solving problems. It's also very rewarding to receive honors, give speaking engagements, and to be interviewed for a book on property management!

**Q:** What is the biggest opportunity you see for new property managers?

**A:** New property managers will be challenged to provide a menu of services tailored to individuals who want to manage their own properties, like showings, credit applications, and lease paperwork. Owners want to be involved but don't fully understand the laws and how complicated the industry has become. Property managers should demonstrate how they can truly enhance the value of an owner's investment, and then stand behind their promise every day.

# 39

*"I have a high degree of integrity – if I say I am going to do something, then I do it."*
Joseph Lacko, JL Management

## BACKGROUND

Joseph Lacko lives in San Clemente, California. He is the primary property manager, facilities manager, and project manager for JL Management. The company has been in business for more than 18 years and has over 150 clients. Their portfolio is comprised of 10 shopping centers and six residential properties in Reno, Las Vegas, and Northern California.

## INTERVIEW

**Q:** How did you get into property management?
**A:** My father started JL Management as a construction company under another name in the early 1980's, and later established the property management arm of the business. I started doing odd jobs for him when I was 13, and I've been a full-time employee for about 10 years.

**Q:** Did you have a mentor?
**A:** My co-mentors were my dad, Joe, and his partner, Bob Grimmick. Bob has been with the company for almost 30 years and was a major influence on my understanding of the business.

**Q:** Are there any educational classes you have taken that have proved to be particularly valuable to you?
**A:** I've always felt that the field work is the most important training ground for property management, but I've also taken quite a few California real estate courses. The most valu-

able ones deal with writing real estate contracts – that's one aspect of property management that's difficult to learn on the job.

**Q:** Any other resources you would recommend?
**A:** The International Council of Shopping Centers (ICSC) is the best resource for commercial property management. Being a member gives us valuable ways to expand, get major tenants, and maintain key relationships with brokers and other property managers.

**Q:** How do you use the Internet to help you in your property management business?
**A:** Managing properties from a distance is a lot easier now with e-mail communication and photo attachments; we can review work that needs to be done or has just been completed. We've also used Craigslist to advertise vacancies, and LoopNet.com for some smaller shop deals. LoopNet was hard to navigate and we haven't used it much, but Craigslist has been surprisingly effective.

**Q:** Do you use any of the social media tools like Facebook, Twitter, or LinkedIn?
**A:** We don't use Facebook for the company, but I've considered creating a Twitter account when I figure out the direction it would take. My tenants could get quick updates there.

**Q:** Do you use any traditional advertising, like newspapers?
**A:** Somebody finally talked me into using a local newspaper for our new venture with residential homes. I was shocked at how many more responses we got than through Craigslist, and at how quickly we rented the homes. The ads have worked very well for us and are still active and successful, for the residen-

> THE INTERNATIONAL COUNCIL OF SHOPPING CENTERS (ICSC) IS VERY VALUABLE TO BROKERS AND PROPERTY MANAGERS.

tial properties at least.

**Q:** Sometimes that success rate with newspapers seems to be based on the geographic location and demographic. Where were you successful with the newspaper ads?
**A:** It was the high desert: Victorville and Hesperia, California.

**Q:** What do you attribute your success to?
**A:** Integrity – we have always stood by our word, whether it's written or verbal. I learned from my father that if we say we are going to do something, then we do it. The other key thing has been taking a steady pace in the expansion of our business, instead of growing too quickly like other companies around us. They've lost properties due to heavy leverage and outrageous loans, but we've kept our rents and loans realistic, so our vacancies remain steady.

> **IT'S THE RELATIONSHIPS THAT I HAVE THAT KEEP ME PERSONALLY INSPIRED.**

**Q:** When things don't go so well and look a little bit bleak, from where do you draw your strength and inspiration?
**A:** The relationships I have with my office staff and tenants keep me personally inspired. We try to keep each other upbeat by discussing our hardships and challenges openly, and by giving each other feedback on how to handle things when they get tough.

**Q:** Do you have any slogans that you go by or that you use in your company?
**A:** My personal mantra is "Do no harm," which gets me focused on how to create resolutions for conflicts. When two parties both seem to have a good argument, I ask myself if one is more harmful to the other, regardless of what's being said. That often helps guide me to a solution.

**Q:** What's the most important attribute you look for in employees?

**A:** I want somebody who has strong people skills and has them universally. The first thing I look for is how an applicant interacts with me and with others.

**Q:** What are you doing now in property management that you wish you had done sooner?

**A:** Being more diligent with proper communications is very important, especially in commercial management situations. Sometimes e-mail hasn't been the most appropriate way; tenants have protested that they weren't informed through proper means, as detailed in the lease, and we've had to start all over again. You have to pay attention to the end goal and communicate accordingly.

> **I WANT AN EMPLOYEE WHO HAS STRONG PEOPLE SKILLS AND HAS THEM UNIVERSALLY, NO MATTER WHOM HE IS INTERACTING WITH.**

**Q:** What are the biggest mistakes you see new property managers making?

**A:** The biggest mistake for an experienced property manager or a new one is having a lack of humility. People let their ego get in the way of their professionalism, and wind up separating themselves from their clients or their peers— that's a power play, and a failure.

**Q:** What are some of the biggest challenges that you face?

**A:** Trying to keep a tenant's spirits up when he's struggling to make ends meet is a challenge, but I try to help the best way I can. I want everybody to succeed, and I never want to lose a client.

**Q:** Are there any tips or tricks that you use to prevent yourself from repeating the same mistake?

**A:** You've got to remember your mistakes to avoid them the next time, but you can't beat yourself up over them and let them haunt you.

**Q:** What is the most rewarding aspect of your property management business?
**A:** I like the variety of things that come my way; I really like to problem solve, and that's what the day-to-day work of property management is all about. Whether it's landscaping issues or parking lot usage, I love to troubleshoot and get things back to a standard mode of operation as quickly as possible. That gives me more satisfaction than any other job I have ever had.

> **MY BIGGEST CHALLENGE IS TRYING TO KEEP A TENANT'S SPIRITS UP WHEN HE IS STRUGGLING.**

**Q:** What do you see as some of the biggest opportunities for new property managers, especially in the commercial space?
**A:** The biggest opportunity is to understand the situation that the commercial industry is going to be in for the immediate future. Properties will continue to change hands, be foreclosed on, and resold. New owners will need guidance to develop the potential of their properties, make them more appealing, and find new tenants. Property managers who can bring something new to the table will find plenty of opportunities there.

**Q:** Describe for me your best commercial tenant.
**A:** I barely know my best commercial tenant. He doesn't need anything from me; he has the right customer flow, keeps the building and the premises in good condition, and pays his rent on time. It means I've created a great environment for him, and I'm lucky to have a lot of these tenants.

*"Companies fail when they continue doing for too long that which made them successful in the past."*

-John Young

# 40

*"Just keep putting one foot in front of the other; don't give up, just keep going."*
Beth Machen, Machen Advisory Group

**BACKGROUND**
Beth Machen lives in Charlotte, North Carolina. She is the president of Machen Advisory Group, established in 2007 with a focus on commercial property management. Beth has over 21 years of experience in the industry.

**INTERVIEW**
Q: How did you get started in property management?
A: About five years ago some lawyers, who were friends of mine, asked me to manage their father's inheritance. It was mostly commercial and regular office buildings, and industrial warehouses. I realized very early on that I needed some education, so I got my broker's license and joined the Institute of Real Estate Management (IREM). I then got my Certified Property Manager (CPM) designation.

Q: Are you doing any "green" commercial projects?
A: Leadership, Energy and Environmental Design (LEED) certification is granted by the United States Green Building Council, which is very prominent on the West coast. In fact Portland, Oregon, and some of the other cities out there now require new buildings to be LEED certified. We're extremely excited that our current project is the first one in this region that will be LEED platinum certified, the highest level you can reach. The owner whom we represent is really committed to that goal. It's a 70,000 square foot office building that will feature wind turbines, solar panels, real-time tracking of en-

ergy usage, and three different lighting levels that automatically adjust with natural daylight. It's all tied into the energy management system.

Q: What books, websites or educational resources have you found to be particularly valuable?
A: IREM is great and so is their website. The Building Owners and Managers Association (BOMA) is also very good.

Q: How are you using the Internet to help you in your property management business?
A: The Internet is a tremendous resource; I use it regularly for research, and to keep up with changes from day to day, which is impossible unless you really dedicate time to it. I also sign up for as many weekly or monthly newsletters as I can – they cover all kinds of topics: city-specific information, crime blotters, energy efficiency, and city expenditures, including stimulus fund usage.

> MANY CITIES ON THE WEST COAST, LIKE PORTLAND, NOW REQUIRE NEW BUILDINGS TO BE LEED (LEADERSHIP, ENERGY AND ENVIRONMENTAL DESIGN) CERTIFIED.

Q: Is that how you keep up with changes in laws that might affect property management as well?
A: Absolutely; IREM and BOMA are very big on staying current with legislative issues that affect property management. We attend the yearly IREM conference in Washington, D.C., to lobby for our industry. The realtor association also issues a Washington report, but that's aimed primarily at residential property management.

Q: Do you use any of the social media tools like Facebook, Twitter, and LinkedIn in your property management business?
A: I use LinkedIn and belong to a "green" group there, but I don't really find the others, like Facebook, beneficial yet for

my property management business. I do more face-to-face than Internet networking, which is just my personal preference.

**Q:** Do you do any PR on TV or radio?
**A:** No, I wouldn't even think of using the newspaper or radio. Our website works amazingly well, because it allows people to instantly see references, referrals, and testimonials.

**Q:** What do you attribute your success to?
**A:** Hard work, staying on top of things, and keeping in touch with tenants and clients are all important. It amazes me how some property managers just collect the rent money every month and don't talk to their tenants, vendors, or owners.

**Q:** When things don't go particularly well, from where do you draw your strength and inspiration?
**A:** I have a very strong faith that always seems to guide me to find the right answers. I also call on my peers to ask how they've addressed similar situations, when I need advice. They're my competitors, but we all know each other through IREM and we help each other out.

> IT AMAZES ME HOW SOME PROPERTY MANAGERS JUST COLLECT THE RENT MONEY EVERY MONTH AND DON'T TALK TO THEIR TENANTS, VENDORS, OR OWNERS.

**Q:** Are there any slogans that you or your company uses?
**A:** "Just keep putting one foot in front of the other; don't give up, just keep going," has served me well. There have been times when I've wanted to throw up my hands on a property, or I've gotten so frustrated with an owner I just wanted to say "forget it." But I keep going back to this slogan and things usually do work out. There's always a solution to every problem.

**Q:** What is the best way to attract and retain employees?

**A:** I've learned the hard way that you need to do much more than just interview people. I call their references, conduct a number of interviews and most importantly, I take them out to view some properties. I ask them to tell me what problems they see; if they don't recognize problems when they see them, they won't be very good in this industry.

**Q:** What are the most important attributes you look for in an employee?

**A:** I look for someone with great people skills, because you have to get along with tenants, vendors, and owners. You also have to earn the respect of your maintenance staff, because good maintenance people are extremely hard to find. They need to know that you'll go out there and scrub or paint if you have to. If you just tell them what to do and they never see you willing to do what it takes to get the job done, they'll leave in a heartbeat.

> WHEN I INTERVIEW NEW EMPLOYEES, I TAKE THEM OUT TO SOME PROPERTIES AND ASK THEM TO TELL ME WHAT PROBLEMS THEY SEE.

**Q:** What are you doing now in property management that you wish you had been doing earlier?

**A:** I reach out a lot more to potential clients than I used to. Networking and staying visible are critical. Now, if I see a property that looks like it's been mismanaged and could benefit from my expertise, I'll try to track down the owner and send him an unsolicited proposal. This has gotten some good results and I wish I'd been doing it earlier.

**Q:** What are some of the biggest mistakes you see new property managers making?

**A:** Some new managers think they can sit behind their desks and just collect the rental fees. They don't put themselves out there and visit their properties enough, which is a big,

big mistake.

**Q:** What are some of the biggest challenges that you face?
**A:** Difficult owners and negative people, who don't listen or give you the leeway you need to actually help them, are big challenges. There are many obstacles out there, but you just have to figure out how to turn them around. For example, the economy has been somewhat of a strain, but it has played into my hands in a way – now is the time when property owners are looking for better management. This is my opportunity to convince them that my experience is what they need.

> **THE MOST REWARDING THING IS WHEN YOU TAKE A PROPERTY THAT'S IN BAD SHAPE AND YOU SEE IT TRANSFORMED.**

**Q:** Describe for me your best owners.
**A:** The best owners listen to you, take your advice and let you do your job, because that's what they're paying you for. They understand that their property is an investment and are willing to spend a little money on preventive maintenance.

**Q:** What have been some of the most rewarding aspects of your property management business?
**A:** The most rewarding thing is when you transform a property that's in bad shape; the rental rates increase and it stays occupied because tenants want to live there. This new LEED project we're working on is going to be a challenge and will be so rewarding when we make it happen. We're trying to involve the Boy Scouts so they can do badge work on the project, like identifying plants and helping us build a bridge in the park on the property.

**Q:** What do you see as some of the biggest opportunities for new property managers?

**A:** Facilities management is a big opportunity; I've managed a church and YWCA's, for instance. But owners may need things other than just property management, so new managers should offer a menu of services like preparing budgets, helping with capital plans or construction management, or planning a tenant appreciation party. They should venture out and even work with other companies. I'm working with a gentleman now who has his own very successful retail leasing and management company. Sometimes he gets more projects than he can handle, and will ask me to take them on to help out, even temporarily.

# 41

*"Motivation and persistence are the most important attributes for an employee."*
Andrea Martini, Midland Realty and Development

## BACKGROUND

Andrea Martini lives in Aurora, Illinois. She is a property manager for Midland Realty and Development. The company was started in 2004 and currently has less than 20 employees. Andrea manages 10 retail, office, and industrial properties for 12 clients.

## INTERVIEW

**Q:** How did you get into property management, and did you have a mentor?

**A:** I met one of my bosses through a family friend. I started with the company as an administrator and slowly worked my way into a property management position. My bosses have 30 years of combined experience in the commercial real estate industry. They've both been my mentors, and have helped me grow dramatically in my career.

**Q:** What educational classes have you taken that have been particularly valuable to you?

**A:** The Institute of Real Estate Management (IREM) offers a lot of courses, and provides them online as well. I've taken marketing and leasing retail properties, investment real estate, finance evaluation, managing investment real estate, and human resources for real estate managers. I'm still pursuing a Certified Property Manager (CPM) designation.

**Q:** How do you keep up with all the new and changing laws at the city, state, and federal levels?

A: Upper management does a good job of keeping us informed, especially through weekly meetings. We discuss any new and changing laws that may affect our company or our properties.

Q: Are there any books that you have found to be particularly useful?

A: When I started with the company, one of my first property assignments was an office building. I read IREM's book on office building management, which was very useful in addition to the course materials in the property management classes.

Q: Any other resources that you have found to be particularly valuable to you?

A: IREM has a lot of material on its website you can tap into. For example, they host "webinars" with speakers who discuss various topics like leasing spaces in office buildings and shopping centers.

Q: Are there any associations that you belong to, other than IREM?

A: IREM is the only one I'm very involved with. I have been to a few of the Northern Illinois Commercial Association of Realtors (NICAR) events.

Q: How do you use the Internet to help you with your property management business?

A: I use the Internet for e-mail communication with tenants, because so many commercial tenants prefer that method. With my Blackberry it's very easy to get back to people in a timely manner, even when I'm out of the office. We also offer our owners online access to their financial statements and quarterly reports.

> IREM IS A GREAT ORGANIZATION THAT HAS A LOT OF RESOURCES AVAILABLE TO ITS MEMBERS.

**Q:** Does your company still use any traditional advertising, like newspapers?
**A:** Sometimes, for leasing, we do use traditional ads. Mainly we use the Internet, in particular commercial databases like LoopNet, CoStar and Property Line for listing available space.

**Q:** Does the company do any other types of PR?
**A:** No, we're a pretty small company. My bosses have been in the business for quite some time, and they both have a lot of networks and contacts. We get new properties largely through word-of-mouth, and have had great success with that.

> WE USE COMMERCIAL DATABASES LIKE LOOPNET, COSTAR AND PROPERTY LINE TO LIST OUR AVAILABLE PROPERTIES.

**Q:** What do you attribute your success to?
**A:** I'm very motivated and persistent. I really like networking, and I'm not afraid to ask questions. Education is definitely a part of it too; I attribute much of my success to my B.A. from Northern Illinois University.

**Q:** When things don't go particularly well, from where do you draw your strength and inspiration?
**A:** I draw from my mentors and bosses. We try to focus on things we can improve now so we can be more effective in the future.

**Q:** Do you have any slogans that you or your company uses?
**A:** One that I use is: "When life hands you lemons, make lemonade."

**Q:** How do you attract and retain the best employees?
**A:** Our company philosophy is that we all work very closely together, from upper management to everyone else in the office. Open communication tends to help retain employees. Financials aren't always the main indicator of retaining the

best people, but we've found that rewarding good work is effective.

**Q:** What are the most important attributes for an employee?
**A:** We want motivation and persistence; we look for employees who don't mind going out of their way to do something, or to work extra hours if needed.

**Q:** Is there anything that you are doing now in property management that you wish you had started sooner?
**A:** The educational courses I've taken contributed so much to the knowledge I have right now. I would have taken more of them, and done it sooner.

**Q:** What are the biggest mistakes that you see new property managers making?
**A:** Their biggest mistake is not keeping an open dialogue with property owners, who like to know what's going on. New managers often procrastinate until the last minute to do something or inform an owner about an important situation. I see the same thing with tenants.

**Q:** What do you see as some of the unique characteristics of commercial property management versus residential property management?
**A:** In commercial property management you're dealing with business owners, long-term leases, longer vacancy periods, and tenant build-outs. You have more discretion in choosing the type of tenants you want. In residential management, you're dealing with where people live from day to day, and the likelihood of someone needing assistance at three o'clock in the morning is higher! Work hours are different too; residential managers

> IF YOU ARE ABLE TO HAVE OPEN COMMUNICATION BETWEEN UPPER MANAGEMENT AND EVERYONE IN THE OFFICE, YOU TEND TO RETAIN EMPLOYEES.

tend to work a lot of weekends, while commercial managers are more likely to have a regular work week.

**Q:** What are some of the biggest challenges you face and how do you overcome those challenges?

**A:** In a difficult economic market, we get requests for rent reduction from tenants. Retail tenants are hit particularly hard by economic downturns, and we try to work with them because it's a lot easier and cheaper to keep an existing tenant than to find a new one. We'll consider things like amending leases, giving temporary rent reductions, or extending the lease a year or two so it will benefit both the owners and the tenants.

> WE LOOK FOR EMPLOYEES WHO DON'T MIND GOING OUT OF THEIR WAY TO DO SOMETHING, OR TO WORK EXTRA HOURS IF NEEDED.

**Q:** Any tips or tricks to help you avoid making the same mistakes?

**A:** I pretty much learn my lesson the first time and don't make the same mistake twice. In property management you have to multi-task, and it's easy to get distracted. I try to write everything down as I go along, so that I can deal with all the different situations that arise from one phone call to another.

**Q:** Describe for me your best client/owner and also your best tenant.

**A:** The best client knows his property, its actual value, and how market rates work. A lot of owners want to be really involved even though they've hired a property management company, so a good client doesn't try to micromanage, just lets us do our job. The best tenant is one who keeps me updated about problems, like a roof leak. I'm not at the properties every day, so I need to know about and take care of a situation before it becomes a bigger issue.

**Q:** What is the most rewarding aspect of property management for you?

**A:** It's really rewarding when a tenant calls and thanks you for finding the right person to fix a problem. It's nice to hear, even though you're just doing your job. I've received "thank you" letters and even flowers from a tenant, and that's very rewarding to me.

**Q:** What do you think are some of the biggest opportunities for new property managers?

**A:** Right now there is a big emphasis on "Going Green," and many property managers are still adjusting to that mentality. Going green has a lot of benefits for owners, such as the new tax incentives that save money long-term. And, of course, it benefits the properties long-term as well.

# 42

*"The biggest opportunity for new property managers is to listen and then listen some more."*
Julie Muir, Elliott Associates, Inc.

## BACKGROUND

Julie lives in Portland, Oregon and has been in the property management business for 27 years. Julie is a senior property manager for Elliott Associates, Inc., where she has worked for over six years. With over 30 employees and as many clients, the company manages approximately 90 retail shopping centers, comprising of 4.3 million square feet. The properties are located in several Western states, including Oregon, Washington, Alaska, North Dakota, Arizona, Utah and Idaho.

## INTERVIEW

**Q:** How did you get into property management, and did you have a mentor at the time?

**A:** I got into it by accident. I was looking for my first job out of high school, and was referred by one of my teachers to a property management company. About five years later, I had a mentor who took me under her wing, showed me the ropes, and taught me the ethical way to do things.

**Q:** Are there any educational classes that you've taken that you have found to be particularly valuable?

**A:** Actually, since I didn't have a college education, I've been like a sponge throughout my career, trying to gather as much knowledge as I could. I did take some college level speech and accounting courses, which helped me a great deal, but the Institute of Real Estate Management (IREM) had all of the perfect classes for me.

**Q:** Are there any recommended blogs, websites, or other educational resources that you found particularly valuable?

**A:** IREM has great publications which are specific to all types of management properties: apartments, offices, retail, and industrial. They also offer some great self-improvement books and courses.

**Q:** Have you been involved in any professional organizations?

**A:** I managed residential properties for 12 years, and was involved in a great local housing association called Metro Multifamily. I was a member of the 82nd Avenue Business Association for a short time; it was a wonderful resource for business owners in a notoriously high-crime area. I'm also involved in IREM both locally and nationally, and the networking opportunities are an excellent way to obtain other points of view, or ask for help on handling something. However, with any professional organization, you only get out of it what you put into it, which makes volunteering really important.

> **WITH ANY PROFESSIONAL ORGANIZATION, YOU ONLY GET OUT OF IT WHAT YOU PUT INTO IT, WHICH MAKES VOLUNTEERING SO IMPORTANT.**

**Q:** How has the Internet helped you in your property management business?

**A:** I can't express enough how much the Internet has helped me in my career. At the push of a button, with Google Earth I can see a property from the air, measure the outside walls, see a tree that needs to be trimmed, or look at new properties we're managing. The Internet has expanded our research and information capabilities; for example, Craigslist.org has helped me find service providers in outlying areas in Alaska.

**Q:** Have you used any of the social media tools like Facebook, Twitter, or LinkedIn?

A: We use Twitter, inviting our clients to follow us on topics related to real estate. We also advertise our company successes there.

Q: What do you attribute your success to?
A: I've taken advantage of a lot of opportunities, and I try to grow every single day by learning something new, soaking in knowledge from peers and supervisors. It took a lot of determination, and now I have the job of my dreams. I've been able to use what I've learned to train others as well, which has been extremely rewarding. Being the person in the middle, I'm like a mediator between owners and tenants. I have to look at both sides to ensure each party walks away feeling that I treated him with respect, and did everything I could to make things right. Communication with my tenants and clients is extremely important.

> I HAVE THE JOB OF MY DREAMS.

Q: When things get particularly bleak, where do you draw your strength and inspiration from?
A: You're always putting out fires in this business, so it can seem negative: phone calls from unhappy tenants, deals gone sour, the economy – it's depressing sometimes. You have to identify the small successes that come along, and acknowledge them. I'm also a big jokester around here, constantly trying to make people laugh and not take things too seriously. That helps a lot.

Q: Are there any slogans that you or your company uses?
A: "Happy tenants equal happy clients." It's really all about choosing a positive attitude. I wrote an article about that, for an IREM publication. Attitude is a choice that only you can make. You can choose to be a grumbler, or you can choose to persevere, keep your head up, and look at every challenge as a learning opportunity. I received a lot of response to that

article.

**Q:** How does your company attract and retain the best employees?

**A:** By being the best. There are companies out there that do a great job, but we do it better. We highly promote the way we manage properties, and we value our clients. Being the best also accounts for our employee retention record. We have clients and employees who have been with us for 20 years or more, still going strong.

> **HAPPY TENANTS EQUAL HAPPY CLIENTS.**

**Q:** What are the most important attributes you look for in employees?

**A:** They can have all the skills in the world, but if they're not eager to learn and to grow, and have some initiative, then I really don't want them. They must have excitement and eagerness about this industry.

**Q:** What are you doing now in property management that you wish you had done sooner?

**A:** We should have looked more closely at our advertising (or lack thereof). We recently revamped our logo and our entire image, created new advertising campaigns that really paid off and made people aware of us. Looking at the benefits now, I think we should have done that a long, long time ago.

**Q:** What are some of the biggest mistakes you see new property managers make?

**A:** Many of them try to make their own mark and end up reinventing the wheel. They are like a bull in a china shop and need to slow down, ask more questions, and learn from others without letting their egos get in the way. They think that they can do it all on their own, but if they gain the support and respect of their supervisors and colleagues, they'll be successful.

**Q:** What are some of the biggest challenges that you face and how do you overcome these challenges?

**A:** Our industry is very fast-paced. It's easy to get so busy you find yourself caught off guard, trying to do more work well with less and less, letting things slip through the cracks. Sometimes you have to stop for a moment, take a breath, and look at the whole picture. We all work as a team, and stay as educated as possible to be expert advisors to our clients. Being involved with real estate associations has helped me a great deal in overcoming many of these challenges.

**Q:** Describe your best client and your best tenant.

**A:** My best client is one who doesn't have unrealistic expectations as a real estate owner. He knows how a property should be maintained, how tenants should be treated, and that there will be ups and downs for which he has to be prepared. The perfect tenant, on the other hand, understands what his lease says. No matter how much we encourage them to get an attorney to read the lease from front to back, so many people just sign it without a clue. Then, a year down the road, they don't understand why they're getting another bill. It saves a lot of frustration if tenants know what's in the lease.

> **THE PERFECT TENANT UNDERSTANDS WHAT HIS LEASE SAYS.**

**Q:** What has been the most rewarding aspect of your property management business?

**A:** Being able to teach and inspire others is fabulous. It makes it all worthwhile.

**Q:** What do you see as some of the biggest opportunities for new property managers?

**A:** New managers should take every opportunity to learn, learn,

learn! Listen, and then listen some more. There are a lot of resources for them to take the initiative and seek out knowledge rather than have it handed to them. They should be eager to be successful and to do a fantastic job for their clients. That will create huge opportunities for them.

# 43

*"The biggest opportunities for property managers are in single-family and vacation homes."*
Russell Munz, Pyramid Real Estate Group

## BACKGROUND

Russell Munz lives in Stamford, Connecticut. Russell is a co-owner and the chief operating officer of Pyramid Real Estate Group, which was established in 1972 and currently employs 25 people. The company manages 75 community associations and 20 commercial mixed-use buildings.

## INTERVIEW

**Q:** How did you get into property management?

**A:** My dad was a real estate appraiser and a construction loan reviewer, which got me very interested in real estate. At Cornell I majored in business, taking classes in hotel management, property management, and real estate finance. After leaving the Army as a captain, I decided to get into a small business that focused on real estate, and became a property manager.

**Q:** Did you have a mentor at the time you got into property management?

**A:** My current partner, Michael Gray, was a great mentor who helped me understand the business of property management for residential and commercial properties, leases, brokerage, maintenance and construction. He's been in the field since 1972; I joined the company in 2001 and it's been a real education, experiential learning with a coach.

**Q:** Are there any books, publications, or educational classes that you have found to be particularly valuable to you?

A: The property management and real estate classes at Cornell were beneficial. The Institute of Real Estate Management (IREM) and Community Association Institute (CAI) also have some great publications and books.

Q: How do you keep up with all the laws that affect your property management business?

A: Our law firm helps us stay on top of things by distilling information on upcoming laws into a paper for me. We're members of the Connecticut CAI, which is very active and provides training programs on proposed laws that govern community association management.

> **IREM HAS SOME GREAT PUBLICATIONS AND BOOKS.**

Q: How does your company use the Internet to help you with your property management business?

A: We have invested in Internet systems that provide more interaction and transparency for our clients. People can pay their rent and common charge statements online; property bills are scanned and posted so clients can be part of the approval process, giving them a better sense of control. We e-mail financial reports to our clients on a monthly basis, and use our website as a portal to showcase properties that are either for rent or for sale.

Q: Do you use any third party websites to do additional advertising?

A: Yes, I've used AdWords on Google ("pay-per-click"), and I've done paid advertising with Yahoo. Both of these have been valuable in generating leads for us.

Q: Does your company use any of the social media tools like Facebook, LinkedIn, or Twitter?

A: We have a LinkedIn profile.

**Q:** What do you do in the way of PR for the company?

**A:** I use traditional press to provide updates on the market and my company, such as local newspapers, the *New England Real Estate Journal*, and *Common Interest*, which is a community association magazine for the state of Connecticut.

**Q:** Do you use any traditional advertising like newspapers?

**A:** No, it's expensive and I get little to no benefit, although I maintain good relations with newspaper editors and writers to be a resource for their real estate related content or questions. My focus has been on PR. I personally write eight to 12 articles per year about property management and real estate, some of which are published in the local magazine for community association management.

> **I ESTABLISH GOOD RELATIONSHIPS WITH NEWSPAPERS, EDITORS, AND WRITERS TO BE A RESOURCE FOR ANY REAL ESTATE RELATED QUESTIONS OR CONTENT THAT THEY NEED.**

**Q:** Didn't you also write a property manager's guide that you put online?

**A:** Yes, I recently wrote *The Quick Start Property Manager Program*. It's a training and business start-up kit for property managers. I put what I've learned in the last nine and a half years into an easy-to-read book, including management agreements, marketing materials, forms, and checklists. I've sold it all around the country as a practical "how-to" resource for getting into property management quickly, and benefiting from my mistakes and successes.

**Q:** What do you attribute your success to?

**A:** First, we're accountable and have a "Can Do!" attitude. We deliver on the promises we make about our services. Second is responsiveness; I've got great staff members who handle our customers' questions and resolve their problems as quickly as possible. Third is hiring those great employees in the first place; we do charge a little bit more for our services because we have better people.

Q: When things don't go particularly well and things are looking a little bleak, from where do you draw your strength and inspiration?
A: If I'm having a tough day, I'll think about my grandparents. One side of the family immigrated here and made it through World War II; on the other, my grandfather worked his way up from bank runner to bank president. I'll remember what my family members went through and my problems will seem relatively small.

Q: Do you or your company operate by any particular slogans?
A: "We're on it." When somebody calls in with a problem, right away we're on the case and taking care of it for him.

Q: How do you attract and retain the best employees?
A: I am always looking for ways to take care of our employees and to help them be successful. Those tools can include more educational opportunities or training events. Prospective employees see what is happening at our company and want to be a part of it; very few employers really take the time to develop their staff.

> **I ATTRIBUTE MY SUCCESS TO BEING ACCOUNTABLE, HAVING A "CAN DO!" ATTITUDE, BEING RESPONSIVE, AND HIRING GREAT PEOPLE.**

Q: What's the most important attribute you look for in an employee?
A: I look for people who have a desire to help others, because that's my main motivation in life.

Q: What are you doing now in your property management business that you wish you had done sooner?

**A:** It took longer than I wanted to provide an online payment solution for our clients. I've also taken a course and read the book, *Topgrading* by Bradford D. Smart, to learn interviewing techniques and improve my chances of hiring only "A" players for my team.

**Q:** What are the biggest mistakes that you see new property managers make?

**A:** Property management is basically a "flat fee for services" business. Some new managers may have trouble setting proper boundaries with clients. They'll want to go above and beyond what's in the management agreement, but not confront the client when something requires an outside resource or additional compensation. They wind up being taken advantage of and getting burned out. New managers need to set expectations and boundaries that are fair to both parties, and stick to them.

> **THE BIGGEST MISTAKE NEW PROPERTY MANAGERS MAKE IS NOT SETTING PROPER BOUNDARIES WITH CLIENTS.**

**Q:** Do you have any tips or tricks that you use so that you don't repeat the same mistakes?

**A:** Training is essential for consistency in operational procedures. I wrote up the standards, and on a monthly basis we review them and train managers and employees. This way new hires know where to go for answers, and how things are done; current employees have a better understanding of how to provide our services on a consistent basis.

**Q:** Have you ever had a chance to read Michael Gerber's, *The E-Myth Revisited*?

**A:** Yes. It's exactly what I went through, a valuable road map for me and for anyone wanting to grow his business. I just sent one to a landscaper looking to take his company to the next level, and I give a copy to every new entrepreneur that I meet.

**Q:** Describe for me your best client.
**A:** My best client wants great service and is willing to pay a premium for it. We want clients who appreciate what we do and will take advantage of our services, like our numerous online tools. Feeling valued for what we provide is great for employee morale.

**Q:** What has been the most rewarding aspect of your property management business?
**A:** Seeing an idea grow from five clients into a continually improving, successful business.

**Q:** What do you see as some of the biggest opportunities for new property managers getting into the business?
**A:** The easiest and most abundant opportunities will be twofold. Single-family homes offer a resource when people have to relocate but can't sell their house; a rental is ideal because someone can occupy and look after it for them. Vacation homes are more common now because of low-interest rate loans and present opportunities for rentals as well. There's a good volume of work in these areas with little competition from a property management stand-point. I outline this and more examples in my training program for property managers.

**Q:** What types of business models are there for property management?
**A:** Property management, traditionally, is a relatively low profit margin business. If you want to grow your company and really see it pay off, you need to add areas of revenue. For example, you can offer brokerage or maintenance services. This strategy also allows you to improve responsiveness and quality control, giving your customers a better value and experience.

## *"Don't risk what you're not willing to lose."*
### Patti Oriot, Maui Markets

### BACKGROUND
Patti Oriot lives in Maui, Hawaii, and has been in property management since 1996. She is the owner of Maui Markets, which specializes in managing condos, vacation rentals, and absentee owner homes. In addition to managing properties, Patti does consulting on marketing, evaluating properties for suitability, and how to set up properties for the vacation rental market.

### INTERVIEW
**Q:** How did you get started in property management?
**A:** In 1996, I was managing restaurants when I met some owners who asked me to manage their homes across the United States, including one in Hawaii. I worked with that family for quite a while, and when I came to Hawaii I started branching out and working for other individuals here. I eventually became the manager of a 200-unit apartment complex before getting a job with a high-end vacation rental company.

**Q:** What educational classes have you taken that have been particularly valuable to you?
**A:** I would say all the classes that I have taken on property management were valuable, including the online courses I took on management and related laws. I also joined the Property Management Association (PMA), and attended a real estate school in Hawaii.

**Q:** Any other associations that you belong to?

**A:** I belong to the Association of Apartment Owners (AOAO), which is actually for condominium owners, and to the National Property Management Association (NPMA).

**Q:** How do you use the Internet in your property management business?
**A:** I can't do my work without it. I use the Internet to pull statistics on different aspects of tourism and vacation rentals, bed-and-breakfasts, travel specials to Hawaii, checking median prices for rentals, and tracking my competition. This helps me to target my advertising.

**Q:** Do you use any of the social media tools in your property management business?
**A:** I have used Facebook for advertising because you can tie in geographically to a very specific city and demographic. You don't have to be an Internet guru to figure it out; it's inexpensive and very easy to set up and use. I also encourage my owners to use Facebook.

**Q:** Do you use any national websites for advertising vacation rentals?
**A:** I use VRBO, Craigslist, and various other independent websites.

**Q:** Do you do any traditional advertising, like in newspapers?
**A:** I only do that for certain occasions. For instance, I have clients who specialize in honeymoon condos, so I encourage them to advertise in the bridal section. I also encourage my owners to put ads in Alaska newspapers to entice residents to vacation in Hawaii. Alaskans receive a state government dividend each year, so we want to take full advantage of different advertising media to get them to spend

> **I HAVE USED FACEBOOK FOR ADVERTISING BECAUSE YOU CAN TIE IN GEOGRAPHICALLY TO A VERY SPECIFIC GROUP OF PEOPLE.**

that money here.

**Q:** What do you attribute your success to?
**A:** I've utilized the experience and skills that I gained through all the jobs I have had in my professional career, for example, the customer service skills I learned from my restaurant management experience.

**Q:** When things don't go particularly well, from where do you draw your strength and inspiration?
**A:** The most difficult situation is when owners don't see the reasons for change. Recently with the current market, I had several owners who just wouldn't come down from their normal rental rates. They are very emotionally and personally tied to their places. I let them know that I appreciate their position and understand the value of their beautiful homes, but just go back to the hard line figures and it's easier to deal with them. So where do I get my inspiration or my strength? Well, I'm in Maui, Hawaii! I go to the beach, take a dip in the ocean, and it inspires me; works every time. The next best thing is a hobby, seeing a movie, anything that lets you step away for a while and regroup.

**Q:** Do you have any slogans that you use?
**A:** "Don't risk what you're not willing to lose."

**Q:** In the past, how did you attract and retain the best employees?
**A:** By taking the time to get to know the person, learn about his dynamics and personality. I generally ask non-work related questions because this is a person you're going to bring into a trusted position. I talk to interviewees about their day, their week, and their life. Then I integrate the work questions as we go.

**Q:** What are the most important attributes you look for in an employee?

**A:** I want employees with a good, genuine attitude. I look at their coping skills and their general demeanor.

**Q:** What are some of the biggest mistakes that you see new property managers making?
**A:** Trying to take on too much too soon, without really understanding and evaluating exactly how it will affect the owners and their clients. They don't properly develop their processes or their relationships. Anybody can put up a website, throw up a bunch of vacation rentals and start getting reservations. But then they can't deliver good quality service, attention to detail, dedication, and a personal touch.

> **THE MOST IMPORTANT ATTRIBUTES I LOOK FOR IN AN EMPLOYEE ARE ATTITUDE, COPING SKILLS, AND THEIR GENERAL DEMEANOR.**

**Q:** What are some of the biggest challenges that you face, and how do you overcome them?
**A:** My current challenge is the poor economy and its effect on the tourism industry. I have to be very creative in how I drive traffic to the websites to get the rentals that we need.

**Q:** What do you do to avoid making the same mistakes?
**A:** I evaluate each problem that comes up, try to find out where it went wrong, and then correct it. I have learned by experience.

**Q:** Describe for me your best owner and your best guest.
**A:** My best owner doesn't have unrealistic expectations; he is able to let go and let me do my job. The perfect guest is someone who has respect for the house. A good guest is a respectful guest.

**Q:** What have been the most rewarding aspects of your property management business?
**A:** I don't treat people as reservations. I'm always really happy

when my guests leave happy.

**Q:** What do you see as some of the biggest opportunities for new property managers?

**A:** If they are flexible and open-minded, there are many positions around the world for caretaking and property management. They can live virtually for free anywhere in the world. That's an amazing opportunity.

> **MY BEST OWNER DOESN'T HAVE UNREALISTIC EXPECTATIONS, AND IS ABLE TO LET GO AND LET ME DO MY JOB.**

---

**Author's Note:**
Be sure to check out *Appendix D* for Patti Oriot's
***Basic Marketing Tips for Vacation Rentals***

---

*"Shoot for the moon. Even if you miss it you will land among the stars."*

-Les Brown

# 45

*"I attribute my success to integrity and relationship building – I've never lost a client."*
Michael Prochelo, Financial Management Group

**BACKGROUND**
Michael Prochelo lives in Los Angeles, California. Michael is the president of Financial Management Group, which was established in 1995. The company manages over 15 large industrial and retail properties comprised of over a million square feet.

**INTERVIEW**
**Q:** How did you get into property management, and did you have a mentor at the time?
**A:** I started out in investments, with Merrill Lynch. For the next several years I ventured into international and private banking, financing large projects for individuals and entrepreneurs. When I left the bank, a couple of my clients asked me to manage their portfolios and businesses, and that was my start in property management. Those initial clients were also my mentors at the time.

**Q:** Tell me about how you typically put together your various leases.
**A:** We usually use our lawyers for everything, because they keep us current on various laws and provide forms for us to use. We meet with our law firm every year to make sure that we're up-to-date. For our smaller properties and clients, we've created a fill-in-the-blanks form letter that we send out once it has been reviewed by our legal team.

**Q:** So the leases for your bigger clients are typically unique and different for each client?

A: A typical commercial lease for a national tenant, like Bed, Bath & Beyond, can be for a term of 10 to 50 years on a property, so you have to make sure you get everything right going into it. These companies often have their own lease form set up to benefit them wherever possible, so you need to go through it and negotiate. If and when a property is sold, that lease will play a very important role in its profitability, so I strongly recommend using a good real estate attorney – I can't stress this enough.

> **THE TERM FOR A LEASE ON A COMMERCIAL DEAL COULD BE ANYWHERE FROM 10 TO 50 YEARS, SO YOU BETTER GET IT RIGHT, BECAUSE YOU'RE GOING TO HAVE TO LIVE WITH IT FOR A LONG TIME.**

Q: Are there associations that commercial property managers belong to that you have found to be particularly valuable?

A: The International Council of Shopping Centers (ICSC) is very good. They have an international convention every year in Las Vegas, and they hold smaller regional conventions throughout the year. They also offer workshops, speakers, and a lot of classes.

Q: How do you use the Internet to help you in your property management business?

A: We live on the Internet! We use it as an incredible research tool, for communications, and for advertising. We do mailers and offer free reports to attract people to our website, and just recently started a blog. We also do a lot of search engine optimization (SEO) to drive traffic to our website.

Q: What do you attribute your success to?

A: Taking care of my client is very important; I'm not out there to just get a fee. I want his repeat business, so I stress integrity and relationship building. I've never lost a client.

**Q:** When things aren't going so well, from where do you draw your strength and inspiration?

**A:** I draw from myself; you've just got to dig in and keep going forward, don't let things pull you down. There are temporary downturns and some last longer than others, but you know that you're going to come out ahead on the other side.

**Q:** How do you attract and retain the best employees?

**A:** By being fair and creating a nice working environment.

**Q:** What's the most important attribute you look for in an employee?

**A:** Integrity.

**Q:** Are you doing anything now in your property management business that you wish you had done sooner?

**A:** We should have done more marketing. Previously we were strictly a referral-based business, but in the last two years we started marketing to branch out and create a larger property management portfolio that I can sell when I retire.

**Q:** What are the biggest mistakes that you see new property managers making?

**A:** They have to be better informed about the overall vision for a property, in order to make good decisions for their clients. They need to know about its real value, what the owner's intentions are, if there are any favorable zoning changes that could be made, or if they could add more square footage to maximize income.

> **THE INTERNATIONAL COUNCIL OF SHOPPING CENTERS (ICSC) IS A VERY GOOD ORGANIZATION FOR COMMERCIAL PROPERTY MANAGERS.**

**Q:** What are some of the biggest challenges you face and how are you dealing with them?

**A:** Dealing with a deep recession is a real challenge, because a lot of tenants can't afford rent in that situation. You have to be proactive, walk your properties, talk to and listen to tenants, be responsive, and know when to cut a deal. If you really work for your tenant, you'll be working for your client. If the tenant stays, the client/landlord is going to be happy.

**Q:** Describe for me your best tenant.
**A:** The best tenant really understands the market and works with everyone on a win-win basis. He's reasonable and fair in decision-making and in relationships with people.

**Q:** What's been your most rewarding aspect of the property management business?
**A:** Redevelopment projects are great. It's fantastic to see what we start with and where it ends up after the redevelopment effort, and to be featured in the local newspaper. It's very rewarding when we make a property more profitable for its owner, and when that turns out to be good for the community as well.

*"The most important attributes for an employee are a good attitude and a desire to learn and improve."*
Mark Quinn, Banyan Property Management, Inc.

**BACKGROUND**
Mark Quinn lives in West Palm Beach, Florida. He is the president and owner of Banyan Property Management, Inc., which was incorporated in February of 1999 and currently employs 55 people. Mark's company specializes in managing homeowners associations and condominium associations, serving 80 clients.

**INTERVIEW**
**Q:** How did you get into property management?
**A:** I worked my way up to a vice president position with Enterprise Rent-A-Car, and my final position with the company was in the United Kingdom. I had the opportunity to lead a couple of operations during my tenure there, creating and implementing a long-term real estate strategy. This involved locating new properties, handling leases, and opening new locations. I left the company in December 2004 and bought this business from my sister, her husband and another couple.

**Q:** Did you have a mentor at the time?
**A:** A few of my former superiors with Enterprise provided me with professional guidance and served as support during my career transition. I also found mentors in a former partner and the owner of another management company. We share similar business and family philosophies, which has had a positive impact on the business.

**Q:** What education classes have you taken along the way that you have found to be particularly valuable?

**A:** In Florida a license is required to be a property manager, which entails the initial course and annual continuing education.

**Q:** How do you keep up with all the laws that affect your property management business?

**A:** We foster relationships with local attorneys who specialize in serving community associations. As changes come up in statutes, obviously we can read them but we're prevented by law from interpreting them. We consult with the attorneys and then get back to our mutual clients with their interpretation and opinions.

**Q:** Any educational books, resources or websites you would recommend?

**A:** The Community Association Institute (CAI) is our professional trade organization geared towards the homeowners and condominium associations; we use them for our continuing education requirements.

**Q:** How does your company use the Internet to help you with your property management business?

**A:** Our website supports our customers and also provides information to potential new clients. I think the best aspect of our website is the FAQs section, which gives answers to the 20 most frequently asked questions about things like application packages, certificates of insurance, and association governing documents. Our phone system explains that many of our residents' questions can be answered by visiting the website.

**Q:** What are you looking at to improve the PR for your company?

**A:** As a relatively small business, our PR is focused mainly on networking with associated professionals, associations, and various trade groups in our area. These groups serve as a resource but also carry considerable political clout. I also make myself accessible to members of local media outlets when they need help with news stories affecting community associations.

**Q:** Do you still use any traditional advertising, like newspapers?
**A:** Traditional print media such as newspapers and even the Yellow Pages give poor returns. I believe our growth in the near future will come from a strong networking effort focused on reputation and brand awareness, such as the referrals generated from our attorneys and CPA firms.

> **BUSINESS IS GENERATED BY REFERRALS FROM ATTORNEYS AND CPA FIRMS.**

**Q:** What do you attribute your success to?
**A:** As a small business owner, you can't have any greater responsibility than to the people who work for you. I value every member of my staff, because they are the ones delivering the customer service that has created a positive company reputation.

**Q:** When things aren't going particularly well, from where do you draw your strength and inspiration?
**A:** When things get bad, I break the issue down into small steps and then formulate a strategy. I'm a former Marine, and one of the things the Marine Corps taught me was that even in the direst circumstances, the worst thing you can do is to appear indecisive. It doesn't matter if your decision is right or wrong; just make a decision, go forward, and then evaluate your progress.

**Q:** Are there any slogans you use personally or that your company uses to overcome challenges?
**A:** Jack Taylor, the founder of Enterprise, had a company mission statement: "Put your customers first. Take care of your

employees and long-term growth and profitability will follow." I adopted the same philosophy in my company. Although making a fair profit is important, I remain focused on delivering the best possible service to our customers while providing a pleasing work environment for my staff.

**Q:** How do you attract and retain the best employees?

**A:** People are attracted to our company because we run it as a family. I'm hesitant to call them employees because I do take a personal interest in them and their families. When we need to hire, I don't run ads in the paper. We network through our current staff and even vendors; an employee referral that brings in a great team member is the best kind.

> IF YOU PUT YOUR CUSTOMERS FIRST AND TAKE CARE OF YOUR EMPLOYEES, LONG-TERM GROWTH AND PROFITABILITY WILL FOLLOW.

**Q:** What are the most important attributes you look for in an employee?

**A:** The most important attribute we look for is attitude. It's the one thing I can't teach. It doesn't matter how smart he is or how much experience he has; if someone doesn't have the right attitude he's just not going to fit our company.

**Q:** What are the biggest mistakes you see new property managers make?

**A:** They focus exclusively on operations like bookkeeping and not on personal interaction with association board members. The board member's position is a thankless job with nothing but complaints from a minority of the membership. The board typically needs a lot more support and counseling than new property managers fully understand.

**Q:** What are some of the biggest challenges you face right now and how are you overcoming those challenges?

**A:** The financial crisis has created massive collection issues for the associations, and I'm now much more of an expert in collection law and foreclosures than I ever desired! Many of our competitors focus on current issues without considering the future operating environment, but we've pioneered innovative legal and financial strategies. We're trying to help find solutions to our customers' issues rather than relying on the status quo.

**Q:** Any tips or tricks that have really helped you avoid making the same mistakes?

**A:** The people who work in our different departments are the ones who come up with the best solutions to solve our customers' issues without the need to run through a bureaucracy. I leave that authority with them and empower them to make decisions, because they answer the phones, handle the problems every day, and know their customers better than I do.

> **THE BIGGEST CHALLENGE RIGHT NOW FOR US HAS BEEN THE FINANCIAL CRISIS THAT IS CREATING MASSIVE COLLECTION ISSUES FOR THE ASSOCIATIONS.**

**Q:** Describe for me your best association board.

**A:** The best board is a politically stable and longer-serving group; when there are transfers of power, they don't all leave the board at once, requiring a reinvention of the wheel with a completely new board. Good, well-run communities, are the ones who allow us to do our job.

**Q:** What has been the most rewarding aspect of doing property management for you?

**A:** I've been able to take care of our staff in this difficult economy; we haven't had to lay any people off. It's also really gratifying to take a troubled community that nobody else wanted and turn it around. You don't always get thanked for it and sometimes you even get fired, but you know that you've left them better off than when they came to you.

**Q:** How do you decide which associations to take on and, once you do take them on, what are some of the initial areas you focus on?

**A:** We try to determine if they are people of integrity and honesty; if they are not, we won't take them on. When we start managing a new association, we first educate them on best practices, understanding their financial statements, and acting as board members per *Robert's Rules of Order* so they don't get hung up in squabbles. We also get them to rely on the various professionals they pay for advice: attorneys, CPAs, and our company.

> **IT IS REALLY GRATIFYING WHEN YOU CAN TAKE A TROUBLED COMMUNITY THAT NOBODY ELSE WANTED AND TURN IT AROUND.**

# 47

*"We try things; it's okay if it didn't work, we just move on and learn from the experience."*
                                    Kellie Sanders, Village Green

**BACKGROUND**
Kellie Sanders lives in Chicago, Illinois. She is the senior vice president of Village Green, which was established in 1919. The company has about 1,400 employees, called "associates," and manages over 35,000 apartments. Kellie has about 20 years of property management experience, and her portfolio consists of over 20,000 residents.

**INTERVIEW**
**Q:** How did you get into property management, and did you have a mentor at the time?
**A:** I worked full-time when I was in college, and my first job was doing maintenance at an apartment community. Upon graduating, I remained in the property management industry.

**Q:** Any educational classes that you have taken that you have found to be particularly valuable?
**A:** Hands-on application and seeing projects to fruition are still the most valuable means to learn the dynamics of this business. Village Green has its own university with quite a large curriculum to educate our associates internally. The standard classes that students are exposed to in the university environment, like business strategies and financials, provide great fundamentals. But the most tangible educational experience is hands-on and face-to-face.

**Q:** How do you keep up with all the laws that affect your property management business?

A: It's all about staying connected with your colleagues. We have the Chicago Residential Landlord Tenant Ordinance (RLTO), which is very challenging for landlords, and trade organizations like the Chicagoland Apartment Association (CAA) and the National Apartment Association (NAA). Our company engages attorneys who are very familiar with the ordinances on a consultation basis and monthly review. Our area directors, the auditing department and I constantly monitor trade articles and search the Internet for the latest updates.

Q: Are there any other associations that you belong to?

A: I am a board member with both the CAA and the Chicago Chamber of Commerce. Village Green is also very involved with the Loop Alliance in the downtown market (formerly the Greater State Street Council).

Q: Any books that you would recommend?

A: *Good to Great* by Jim Collins and *Women Lead the Way* by Linda Tarr-Whelan.

Q: How do you use the Internet in your property management business?

A: No less than 70% of the traffic for rentals is generated through the Internet; it's the core of our advertising venues. We can track our web hits and monitor productivity; our director of social media oversees our blog, Facebook, MySpace, and Twitter accounts. These tools are incredibly popular with our residents, who can go online to apply, sign a lease, make service requests, tell us how we're doing, learn about community events, and connect with each other. We see ourselves as if we are in the hospitality industry and renting a lifestyle, not just apartments. The Internet provides us with valuable transparency within the company and in relation to our clients.

**Q:** Do you find the effectiveness of the social media tools to be directly related to the age demographic of your populations?
**A:** Absolutely. We have a large demographic that's between 25 and 35 years old.

**Q:** Do you use any traditional newspaper advertising?
**A:** We use very little print media, except for non-traditional approaches that speak to our residents' lifestyle, like group advertising. We may buy a page in the *Chicago Social* which highlights the entire urban portfolio, or identify specific print publications in each suburban market. This has been very successful for us and helped to foster a personal identification for our customers.

> **WE HAVE A POSITION IN OUR ORGANIZATION CALLED THE DIRECTOR OF SOCIAL MEDIA, WHOSE SOLE RESPONSIBILITY IS TO MONITOR OUR FACEBOOK, MYSPACE, AND TWITTER ACCOUNTS, AS WELL AS THE VILLAGE GREEN BLOGS.**

**Q:** Do you do any PR for your company?
**A:** We have our own PR department, and regional marketing directors who are responsible for getting out into the community to create relationships with local businesses and large corporate employers.

**Q:** What do you attribute your success to?
**A:** I've had a lot of ambition, am organized and focused, which is a simple but overlooked strategy. Throughout my career I've kept track of what has worked and what has not worked regarding best practices. And I'm not afraid to tackle complicated tasks head-on, with the mentality that everything is possible.

**Q:** When things don't go so well, from where do you draw your inspiration and strength?
**A:** I try to keep myself and my teams motivated by not focusing

on the negativity of the situation or fear of failure. We try things; we're not afraid to make changes, we move quickly, and it's okay if it didn't work. We just move on and learn from the experience.

**Q:** Are there any slogans that you use?
**A:** For me, it is "Transparency." Transparency is critical.

**Q:** How do you attract and retain the best employees?
**A:** Our unique recruitment and training program has reduced our company's turnover significantly. This "Manager in Training" program is a six-month course for university graduates, with classroom time and on-site training for day-to-day experience. We immerse them in our corporate culture and strong ethics of customer service. At the end of the course, new associates must give an oral presentation to the officers and executive board before graduation and assignment to a property. We've had a very good success rate in productivity and employee retention through this program.

> I ATTRIBUTE MY SUCCESS TO NOT BEING AFRAID TO TACKLE SOME OF THE MORE COMPLICATED TASKS HEAD-ON, WITH THE MENTALITY THAT EVERYTHING IS POSSIBLE.

**Q:** What's the most important attribute you look for in a new employee?
**A:** I look for somebody with ambition, who is going to be a catalyst and make a difference in the organization.

**Q:** What are you doing now in property management that you wish you had done sooner?
**A:** I wish that we'd created our internal benchmarking process sooner. We now have standards in place that used to be more assumed than measured. There are weekly quotas for leasing consultants, service managers, and every associate in our company. At first we had some resistance to the idea

as too aggressive and not possible, but now our associates are continually hitting all the benchmarks. We learned that if you raise the bar high enough and you give people the right tools, the majority of them will succeed. I also wish we had implemented our bonus program earlier. The president, area directors and property managers are given bonuses based on the same criteria: customer satisfaction and asset performance. If we achieve our goals we are rewarded for it as a team, which encourages everybody to work together cohesively and stay aligned to our customers, our owners, and each other.

> **OUR EMPLOYEE TURNOVER RATE IS EXTREMELY LOW FOR OUR INDUSTRY.**

**Q:** What are some of the biggest mistakes that you see new property managers making?
**A:** They struggle with organizing their priorities and calculating what should be done versus what can be done. When they first start, they don't understand how truly complicated and demanding every day can be. New managers need to keep themselves organized, use the resources provided to them and, most importantly, ask for help when they need it.

**Q:** What are some of the biggest challenges that you face and how do you overcome them?
**A:** Trying to, what I call, push the "impossibles." If we do a really good job at something I ask how we can be great at it. I usually approach this by getting the team together for their feedback and ideas. Then we set very specific goals and timelines to figure out how we can conquer it.

**Q:** Describe for me your best resident and your best client.
**A:** In both cases it is someone who pushes us, and who gives us feedback. Obviously a resident who adheres to the lease, respects his neighbors and the community, is very much appreciated. But I also like a resident who gives me feedback,

so we can make continued improvements. We solicit our residents for comments when we're touring with a new prospect, when they move, and with an annual survey. The best client understands this industry and challenges us. I really enjoy the ones who want us to exceed their expectations; it's a challenge that is very rewarding.

**Q:** What aspects of property management have been the most rewarding for you?
**A:** It's extremely rewarding when I see our portfolio grow. What's especially rewarding is seeing my team grow, and the internal promotions they attain.

**Q:** What do you see as some of the biggest opportunities for new property managers getting into the business?
**A:** There really are no limits any more; it's such a vast, diverse, and growing industry. Village Green has so many different branches; it's really limitless as far as the opportunities for career advancement and growth.

# 48

*"Financial skills and people skills are very important in this business."*
Bob Spicker, Colliers International

## BACKGROUND
Bob Spicker lives in San Francisco, California. Bob is the managing director of real estate management services for the San Francisco office of Colliers International, which has operations throughout the United States, Canada, Asia, Australia, New Zealand, Latin America, South America, and Europe. Bob's office was established in 1995 and has 10 employees. They manage 34 small office buildings and one retail center.

## INTERVIEW
**Q:** How did you get into property management?
**A:** After I left corporate real estate I went into consulting. I didn't really like it though, and the company I went to work for was failing. A headhunter I'd worked with previously called me and said, "How about a job in property management?" I got the job even though I didn't know the first thing about it!

**Q:** Are there any educational classes that you have taken that you have found to be particularly valuable to you?
**A:** Ninety percent of the courses that I have taken have been courses offered by the Building Owners and Managers Association (BOMA).

**Q:** How do you keep up with all the city, state, and federal laws that affect your business?
**A:** I use BOMA; the San Francisco chapter is the fourth largest, and this association is very strong when it comes to advocacy

and sustainability.

**Q:** Are there any other associations that you also belong to that have been valuable to you?
**A:** I participate primarily in BOMA, and periodically I attend some functions put on by the Institute of Real Estate Management (IREM).

**Q:** How do you use the Internet in your property management business?
**A:** We use it all the time for communications among our managers. Five of our clients live in Asia, and the only way we communicate with them is through the Internet.

**Q:** What do you use for advertising: the Internet, traditional newspaper ads, or both?
**A:** We use a combination of both.

**Q:** What do you attribute your success to?
**A:** I attribute it to good people skills – this is a people business and a relationship business. But there was also a lot of hard work and some good luck. Financial skills have helped me too. With my degree in accounting, I certainly understand and can relate to the numbers side of the business.

> I ATTRIBUTE MY SUCCESS TO HAVING GOOD PEOPLE SKILLS.

**Q:** When things don't go so well, from where do you draw your strength and inspiration?
**A:** I draw from my faith, and I surround myself with good co-workers whom I can count on. I've been in the business for a long time, so I can also reach out to friends, peers, and superiors for help when I need it.

**Q:** Are there any particular slogans that you use personally or your company uses?

**A:** Our company slogan is "Our knowledge is your property."

**Q:** How do you attract and retain the best employees?
**A:** Obviously a competitive salary and benefits package are important. I find it very difficult to attract and hire good people, so when I find somebody I try hard to keep him. We operate and manage the Class B smaller buildings, so my managers really have to know how to handle virtually everything, from plumbing leaks to budgets and annual expense escalations.

**Q:** What are the most important attributes that you look for in an individual? It sounds like having a broad and diverse set of skills is certainly important.
**A:** Yes, that is really important for me. Financial skills are probably the most important thing, but people skills are critical. Employees have to deal with and get along with all types of people: owners, families, tenants, vendors, and contacts in general.

> **COMPANY SLOGAN:** "OUR KNOWLEDGE IS YOUR PROPERTY."

**Q:** What are you doing now in property management that you wish you had started doing sooner?
**A:** As property managers we could have been further ahead of the curve on sustainability and "green" initiatives. Some of our vendors saw it coming, but we didn't pick up the ball on that and are now scrambling to get more involved.

**Q:** What makes your company unique compared to your competitors?
**A:** We're a big international company but our individual offices operate more as entrepreneurs. The advantage to this is that I have a lot of flexibility in how I handle things based on market and client conditions, while my counterparts at other companies have to act within a corporate structure. We can be more nimble and more able to tailor our services to our

clients' needs, but the disadvantage is not working with the big institutional owners like our competitors do.

**Q:** What are some of the biggest mistakes you see new property managers making?

**A:** They tend to look very narrowly at what their expertise needs to be, and this will tend to reduce their career opportunities in the long term.

**Q:** What are some of the biggest challenges that you are facing right now and how do you overcome them?

**A:** It's very challenging to satisfy a client's desire to reduce expenses, and to find ways to operate our buildings more economically when we're already doing a good job of that. Working closely with my vendors helps. Vacancies are up and rents are down, but you have to find a balance so that you run a good building and continue to attract tenants.

**Q:** Describe your best tenant.

**A:** The best tenant is someone who can create a good working relationship and good rapport; very professional and fair, pleasurable to deal with.

**Q:** What are some of the most rewarding aspects of your property management business?

**A:** I really enjoy it when we get to do things a little bit above and beyond just property management in meeting our client's requirements. Sometimes we get to do asset management work, and it's very rewarding to be involved in an owner's decisions to buy or sell property. It's an opportunity to get out of the day-to-day humdrum.

> **COMPARED TO OUR COMPETITORS, WE ARE MORE NIMBLE AND MORE ABLE TO TAILOR OUR SERVICES TO OUR CLIENTS.**

**Q:** What do you think are some of the biggest opportunities for new property managers?

**A:** Property management is certainly moving to a higher degree of professionalism. The level of expectation, sophistication, and financial acumen required for this job has really increased, and the pay scale has increased considerably to reflect that. There are great opportunities for young people going into this field.

*"Creativity is thinking up new things.
Innovation is doing new things."*
                              -Theodore Levitt

*"Doing the ordinary, extraordinarily well."*
Edward Thomas, Property Management People, Inc.

### BACKGROUND
Edward Thomas lives in Frederick, Maryland and is the CEO of Property Management People, Inc. (PMP). The company was founded by his wife and business partner, Rose, in September 1980, and has 55 employees. They manage approximately 400 properties including single-family homes, town homes, condominium units and some warehouse space. They also manage over 80 homeowner and condominium associations totaling more than 33,000 units in Maryland, Virginia, West Virginia, and Pennsylvania.

### INTERVIEW
**Q:** How did you get into property management?
**A:** We actually started as a traditional real estate sales company and found ourselves in the property management business out of a need to survive. We started the company in 1980 when interest rates soared as high as 18%. Like many realtors in today's similar market, we took on properties as rentals because their owners couldn't sell them. When the market improved, we made a business decision to stay in the property management industry.

**Q:** Have you taken any educational classes that you have found to be particularly valuable?
**A:** I'm a licensed real estate broker, so I have some continuing education there. We really get our education from the professional associations we belong to. I've been involved with

the Community Associations Institute (CAI) since 1984, and earned my professional community associations manager (PCAM) designation from them. Rose took her early classes through the Institute of Real Estate Management (IREM), and subsequently obtained two designations from the National Association of Residential Property Managers (NARPM).

Q: How do you keep up with all the laws that affect your property management business?

A: We both serve on a number of committees and boards within our organizations, and maintain a strong network of professional colleagues. We constantly receive legal updates and law reports from our memberships and subscriptions, and both Rose and I have been fortunate to serve as president of our respective national organizations.

Q: Any books that you've read that you would recommend?

A: Everyone should obtain a copy of a college business law textbook and a law dictionary. The textbook is full of sound business advice and the law dictionary is handier than a phone book. *Good to Great, Trading Up, Boomburbs, Simple Leadership Principles*, and *Selling the Invisible* are all books I've read in the last two years. I also read *The Financial Times*, sections of the *Wall Street Journal*, and our local paper every day. I subscribe to a number of financial services including *Roubini Global Economics, HS Dent, Trends Magazine* and the *Business Briefings*.

Q: Any other websites or educational resources that you would recommend?

A: I subscribe to the semi-annual *Wharton School of Business Real Estate Periodical* reports and continuously refer to the *T2Partners LLC Housing Report*. We monitor the various websites in states where we manage property, and have web links to databases serving each region. I read all the CAI periodicals, about two per month.

**Q:** What do you do for advertising and marketing?

**A:** We use traditional newspaper classified advertising and Craigslist, and we still maintain a Yellow Pages listing. We issue press releases whenever we have newsworthy events, but we have yet to advertise on TV or radio. Remarkably, most of our growth continues to come from client referrals or word-of-mouth. Our advertising budget is predominantly spent on hiring and recruiting.

**Q:** What do you see as the keys to successful property management?

**A:** Integrity, honesty, loyalty and attention to details, a strong work ethic and commitment to both your clients and employees are paramount. I was once an air traffic controller, and at the end of your shift you could walk away from the stress of the job and go home. Being a professional manager is even more stressful because you're involved with it 24/7/365. It takes a strong person, willing to commit to the industry, to be successful.

> **INTEGRITY, HONESTY, LOYALTY AND ATTENTION TO DETAILS ARE THE KEYS TO SUCCESSFUL PROPERTY MANAGEMENT.**

**Q:** What do you attribute your success to?

**A:** Each day we strive to lead by example, to set high but attainable goals for staff members, and maintain a professional and courteous corporate culture. We work long hours, commit ourselves to our clients, try to do what is right, and treat people with respect and dignity. We've established internal standardized operating procedures that are fair and consistent, and place a strong emphasis on continuing education and ethics. We never expect our staff to do something that we haven't done ourselves.

**Q:** When things don't go particularly well, from where do you draw your strength and inspiration?

**A:** We've learned that we are better off addressing issues head on. We schedule a meeting, get with the employee, board members, or property owners, and try to work through the problem politely and professionally. We've learned to separate the emotions from the facts, and I think we've been really successful in finding solutions everyone can live with.

**Q:** Are there any slogans that you use?
**A:** "Doing the ordinary, extraordinarily well."

**Q:** How do you attract and retain the best employees?
**A:** During the interview process we look for attitude and aptitude. Employees must pass a drug screening test and a credit check, and must be eligible for bonding by our insurance carrier. Managers are expected to attend several evening meetings each month, which is the Achilles' heel of the association management business, but we never sugarcoat any position during the interview process. While we will always consider an experienced manager, we've been very successful with people who have good customer service skills, the right attitude, and who want to learn, grow and attain long-term security as a certified professional manager.

> **WE ATTRIBUTE OUR SUCCESS TO WORKING LONG HOURS, COMMITTING OURSELVES TO OUR CLIENTS, TRYING TO DO WHAT IS RIGHT, AND TRYING TO TREAT PEOPLE WITH RESPECT AND DIGNITY.**

**Q:** What is the most important attribute that you look for in an employee?
**A:** We believe a person's past performance is the best indicator of future conduct, and we look for integrity, honesty, loyalty and commitment. We ask interviewees a series of behaviorally based questions, asking them to draw on their work history or personal life experiences for illustrations of how they handled a particular situation. This is even more important

if the outcome wasn't favorable; it provides a unique insight into the person you are considering hiring.

**Q:** What are you doing now in your property management business that you wish you had done sooner?

**A:** For the past year we've been writing detailed operating procedures for each aspect of our business: annual meetings, generating proxies and ballots, financial statements, documents, board reports and inspections. Had we started this years ago, we could have eliminated mistakes and provided a stronger foundation for our staff.

**Q:** What are some of the biggest challenges you face?

**A:** The biggest challenge we face is the current economic climate. Homeowners literally walk away from their properties, associations are financially squeezed by delinquent owners or foreclosures, and good people's credit have been damaged. For our community managers, being out even three to four evenings a month is also a challenge. We typically find that everyone has to compromise, tell the truth, and work through the problems.

> **WHEN WE INTERVIEW PEOPLE, WE ASK A SERIES OF BEHAVIORALLY-BASED QUESTIONS.**

**Q:** Describe for me your best client.

**A:** Our best clients are those who are honest with us, don't expect perfection, recognize the sacrifices our employees make to serve them, and give us feedback.

**Q:** What have been the most rewarding aspects of the property management business?

**A:** The most rewarding thing is to look at a community where we've truly made a positive difference. It's well run, with modest dues, increases every few years and adequately funded reserves; the properties have high curb appeal, and we all work well together. The ultimate reward comes when we obtain unsolicited client referrals.

**Q:** What do you see as the biggest opportunity for new property managers entering the field?

**A:** I see a growing trend with state manager licensing. As communities mature and get larger, it takes an ever-increasing degree of knowledge, experience, education and sophistication to manage them. We have to be lawyers, leaders, and diplomats, read financial statements, have strong communication skills, deal with conflict resolution, and still keep a positive attitude – every business day. People who are willing to come in, pay their dues, commit themselves to the industry and to learn, will never be without a job. Whenever people leave our company to relocate, I've been able to pick up the phone and find them a job in their new city. That type of network doesn't exist in every profession.

> **THE PEOPLE WHO ARE WILLING TO COME IN, PAY THEIR DUES, COMMIT THEMSELVES TO THE INDUSTRY AND TO LEARN, WILL NEVER BE WITHOUT A JOB.**

*"We look for our employees to have integrity, honesty, and self reliance."*
Nigel Worrall, Florida Leisure Vacation Homes

### BACKGROUND
Nigel Worrall lives in Kissimmee, Florida. Nigel has been the owner of Florida Leisure Vacation Homes since 1997. He manages approximately 80 vacation rental homes, 10 long-term rental properties, and one commercial building which in total is worth approximately $25 million.

### INTERVIEW
**Q:** How did you get into property management?
**A:** We had a business in the United Kingdom and started vacationing in Florida on a regular basis. We fell in love with the state and purchased a home in Orlando, close to Disney World, which we rented out when not using it ourselves. After a few years we decided to relocate to Florida permanently, and bought the property management company which became Florida Leisure Vacation Homes.

**Q:** What educational classes have you taken that have proven to be very valuable to you?
**A:** I became a full-time student of marketing and real estate, and got my real estate license. I've taken so many courses it's hard to list them. I have comprehensively studied both the short-term and long-term rental laws in Florida. These are essential tools for any property manager here to master.

**Q:** How do you keep up with all the new laws related to property management?

**A:** I attend courses, read the new laws as they're enacted, subscribe to several e-mail services related to real estate, and I read many blogs on these subjects.

**Q:** Any books, websites, or other educational resources that you would recommend?

**A:** First, you have to study the human mind and understand human behavior. One of the best resources for that is *Psycho-Cybernetics* by Maxwell Maltz. I recommend Napoleon Hill's *Law of Success*, and Michael Gerber's excellent book called *The E-Myth Revisited*, which describes how to run a business and how to work on it, not in it. I have a mentor, Dan Kennedy, who helped me understand how absolutely essential marketing is. It's also quite useful to attend meetings and talk with like-minded entrepreneurs and business partners.

**Q:** What are you reading now?

**A:** *Why People Don't Buy Things*, by Harry Washburn and Kim Wallace; I'm re-reading *The Starbucks Experience* by Joseph Michelli and Dan Kennedy's *No B.S. Marketing to the Affluent*.

**Q:** Do you participate in any professional organizations?

**A:** For several years I've been active as a member, board member, or president of many organizations: the Central Florida Property Managers Association (now called Central Florida Vacation Rental Managers Association), two homeowner associations in the Central Florida area, the Realtor organization, and the Florida Association of Residential Property Managers. They have been invaluable in terms of support and further education. It's up to me, as a member of such groups, to use what they have to offer and not rely on them

> **I HAVE COMPREHENSIVELY STUDIED BOTH THE SHORT-TERM AND LONG-TERM RENTAL LAWS IN FLORIDA, AND THESE ARE ESSENTIAL TOOLS FOR ANY PROPERTY MANAGER TO MASTER.**

to come to me.

**Q:** Do you use any of the social media tools like Facebook, Twitter, or LinkedIn?

**A:** Absolutely, these tools are extremely valuable for creating relationships and entering the conversations in people's minds. So many people on Twitter use it only as an advertising medium, but that's the wrong approach. Selling yourself comes later, but you have to create a personal relationship first, which you can do extremely well by using social media in the correct way.

> A LOT OF PEOPLE SEND OUT PRESS RELEASES BUT THE MEDIA WON'T PUBLISH THEM IF THE STORY ISN'T INTERESTING TO THEIR READERS.

**Q:** Do you do any traditional advertising, like newspapers?

**A:** Traditional advertising is helpful when it's done right. Everything has to be tracked and measured. Only then can you know what medium is working and what isn't working.

**Q:** Do you do any PR for your company?

**A:** PR is another very important area of the marketing equation and shouldn't be ignored. It needs constant attention, and you have to have a compelling story to tell. The media won't publish your press releases if the story isn't interesting to their readers.

**Q:** What do you attribute your success to?

**A:** A lot of my success is due to the fact that I'm always ready, willing and able to try something different, which puts me ahead of the pack most of the time. I also listen, learn, and implement. Many people take courses, buy tapes, CDs, DVDs, but then they fail to use the information in a constructive way.

**Q:** Is there a particular slogan that comes to mind to help you overcome challenges?

**A:** My current favorite that I point out often to my staff is "I am a man of simple tastes, easily satisfied with the best," by Winston Churchill. There are many quotes and slogans I enjoy from people like Jim Rohn and Zig Ziglar.

**Q:** How do you attract and retain the best employees?

**A:** We have very specific systems in our company relating to front desk, marketing, sales, maintenance, organization, and accounting. This keeps us on track and empowers everyone to do his job. We don't have a problem attracting or keeping employees because we always encourage them to grow, and we don't micromanage.

> **I ATTRIBUTE MY SUCCESS TO BEING WILLING TO LISTEN, LEARN, AND THEN IMPLEMENT.**

**Q:** What are the most important attributes you look for in an employee?

**A:** We look for integrity, honesty, self-reliance, and the ability to do the job. We don't want people who are afraid to take personal responsibility for their actions and situations.

**Q:** What are you doing now in your property management business that you should have started doing sooner?

**A:** We do a lot more now from a marketing point of view, which we should have done much sooner. In fact, our whole focus has changed from being a property and vacation rental management business to being a marketing business. Now we're seeing more repeat customers, approximately 3,000 guests who come back and visit us time and time again.

**Q:** What are the biggest mistakes you see new property managers make?

**A:** So many new managers have severe cash flow problems and go out of business after a short time, because they don't plan for the future and don't understand the importance of marketing to attract the right type of client. I became so concerned about what was happening to the industry and our public image as a whole that I created a training course called "Property Management Mastery." Just recently the vacation rental industry commissioned a report that showed that our economic impact on the Orlando area was over four billion dollars.

> **THE WHOLE FOCUS OF OUR BUSINESS HAS CHANGED FROM BEING A PROPERTY MANAGEMENT AND VACATION RENTAL BUSINESS TO BEING A MARKETING BUSINESS.**

**Q:** What are some of the biggest challenges you face?
**A:** Consumers no longer trust big business, and want to know that the company they are dealing with isn't going to rip them off, waste their time, or make life harder. They want to know that we understand their unique needs, desires, pressures, and lifestyles. They want to know, like, and trust us before they will commit to buying from us, and getting that message of trustworthiness across is challenging.

**Q:** How have you overcome those challenges?
**A:** We do it by working smarter and by developing better relationships with our customers. We have to get out of our comfort zones and get back to talking to people more, to find out what they want and not deliver what we think they want.

**Q:** Any tips or tricks that have really helped you to avoid repeating the same mistakes?
**A:** We document things when they go wrong and then work together as a team to resolve the issue. We don't want it to happen again, but we can give a better response if it does.

**Q:** Describe some of your best clients.

**A:** The best vacation guest is typically a reasonably affluent individual who values family and enjoys life. He expects a certain quality of vacation home and a high level of service, from first contact through the whole experience of staying with us. The best vacation homeowner understands that his property is effectively the same as a small hotel. He realizes that the property must be maintained at a very high level and isn't afraid of spending money to do so. The best rental resident is honest with us even when experiencing difficulty and unable to pay rent on time. Our ideal tenant holds the same values as we do: honesty, integrity and self-reliance. The best residential property owner is prepared to be patient and understanding when things don't go smoothly. He also knows the value of maintaining his investment property to a high standard.

> **THE MOST REWARDING ASPECT OF MY PROPERTY MANAGEMENT BUSINESS IS BEING ABLE TO SERVE PEOPLE AND TO MAKE THEIR DREAMS COME TRUE WHEN VACATIONING IN ORLANDO.**

**Q:** What have been the most rewarding aspects of your property management business?

**A:** It's wonderful to see the reactions of people when they find a vacation rental home to be well above their expectation level. Serving people and making their dreams come true is very fulfilling, and when your efforts are appreciated it makes you want to do things even better.

**Q:** What do you see as some of the biggest opportunities for new property managers?

**A:** There are some great opportunities for individuals who want a career that can be very rewarding. Companies like ours are always looking for intelligent people who can bring something new and different to the industry.

# APPENDIX D

### BASIC MARKETING TIPS FOR VACATION RENTALS
by Patti Oriot

The best of everything isn't anything if no one knows about it. How many times have you discovered an amazing place, food or item that, unbelievably, isn't in the mainstream of things? Marketing is the key ingredient to the success of any project. Retail or rentals, it all comes down to creating effective advertising techniques, and connecting with your niche in the market place.

The public has been conditioned to respond to advertising. Some people still respond to a basic listing, but this has become a challenging market. Just placing a listing on Vacation Rentals by Owner (VRBO.com) isn't enough any more. The creative owner is the one who will survive these times.

**STEP 1:** *Evaluate your product. Make a list of what it needs. Make your product ready.*
The first step is evaluation of what you have to offer. Your vacation rental should be test-marketed just like any product. Stay a night yourself, as if you were the guest. When you approach the property, is the path well lit and clear of debris, is the front door clean, does the key go in smoothly, is the address legibly displayed, did you send the guest clear driving instructions prior to his arrival? Fix any problems and make your product ready. You never want to have an unsatisfied guest. With the tremendous effect that the Internet has, bad press can be damaging or fatal to your business.

**STEP 2:** *Comparison-shop and find your niche market.*
After you have inspected and prepared your property, identify your market. Many owners advertise in the main newspaper or the most popular local publication, thinking they will get results just based on the number of subscriptions. This will do you no

good if your market is not reading that publication!

Are you targeting a high-end market, families, brides, or corporate? Is your place a "destination" resort close to a tourist area or historical attraction? Have you done your math to figure out exactly what you need to charge in order to make a profit? Many owners right now are only able to maintain a break-even point. Have a plan in place for moving beyond break-even; be prepared to make a profit when the time is right. You have to find the market that is looking for you, even ones you haven't thought of! Only you will know if they are right for your type of property. In the evaluation process, note the amenities that are provided for the guests. If you are marketing to families, does the property have sufficient age-appropriate games, movies, pool toys, and books? Is there a generous supply of local books, guides and up-to-date magazines about the area? Have you provided a list of suggestions for a rainy or bad weather day?

When searching for how and where to market your property, take the time to "shop" the area and the competition's ads. Read ads for similar properties with the eyes of a prospective guest. Is there enough information? Do they make you want to keep reading? Are the photos of good quality and angles? Are all your questions answered? Could you see yourself staying there? Is it a good value? Are there any reviews?

**STEP 3:** *Prepare your marketing budget. Create appealing, easy-to-understand ads.*
Once your marketing budget is established, decide where you will get the most for your money. Sometimes you have to spend more on a one-time ad in order to capture a limited market. This is the case with a holiday vacation guide, pull-out bridal section, or a publication geared to local conventions or events needing a large number of accommodations.

Make sure that you don't go overboard in your advertising either. I've seen ads with so much going on that I couldn't even figure out exactly what the offer was!

**STEP 4:** *Use the Internet as a means to market.*
Try to use as much free marketing as you can! Craigslist is a great free marketing tool, and posting to Craigslist in your guest's hometown is always a good idea. Facebook has low-cost ads as well. You can select to pay per click, which means that thousands of people may see your ad but you only pay for the clicks to your site. Many vacation rental owners use VRBO.com. This is a very good site, but your success depends on what the copy says about the place, the quality of the photos and the promptness of the inquiry response. Most clients want to know almost instantly if your place is going to work for them. Don't forget they are usually trying to coordinate flights.

Internet marketing is a great way to reach a mass market, but do your homework and make sure that the site you're going to use is a reputable one with a successful history. You can find out who owns the website by going to www.WhoIs.com on the Internet, as long as the owners did not make their information private, and you can also search for other public information. Another free marketing tool that is often overlooked is reciprocal links with other sites. Just make sure that the links you place on your site are applicable to your guests' use, and that they are active. Many times I have clicked on "dead" links on sites.

If you are going to use print media, build a relationship with the advertising representatives. They are usually willing to give reductions off the rate schedule if you regularly place ads with them. This is especially helpful if you market for more than one property.

**STEP 5:** *Follow up with former guests.*
Previous guests are also a great marketing tool; don't forget about them after they are gone! Maintaining a client portfolio is a must. Send out an e-mail quarterly with an incentive to return. Make the offer transferrable in the event your previous

guests cannot use it, but may have friends or family who can. Always follow up with your guests, and ask for input from their stay if they did not fill out a guest comment sheet or sign your guest book.

**STEP 6:** *Be consistent with your marketing.*
Don't despair if your first attempts at marketing your vacation rental bring you limited results. Many times someone will see an advertisement and not act on it until weeks or months down the line. Keeping current with your marketing will ensure that you are laying a good foundation for your marketing plan.

**STEP 7:** *Other tips and suggestions.*
Always have brochures or information regarding your rental with you. Every day is a good day for marketing! Do what you can but don't hesitate to hire a professional. This is money well spent for your rental investment.

Marketing vacation rentals or rental properties does require some specific guidelines and familiarity with every aspect in order to advertise successfully. Get a copy of the rental contract and go over it. You wouldn't want to market a condo as "perfect for a romantic weekend" if there is a minimum stay of four nights. Start small and don't take on more than you can handle. You want to be effective and efficient.

Keep the guests' perspective in view at all times.

## RECAP

**Here is a starter checklist, if you need a little direction in getting started:**

**Step 1:** Evaluate your product. Make a list of what it needs. Make your product ready.
**Step 2:** Comparison-shop and find your niche market.
**Step 3:** Prepare your marketing budget. Create appealing, easy-to-understand ads.
**Step 4:** Use the Internet as a means to market.
**Step 5:** Follow up with former guests.
**Step 6:** Be consistent with your marketing.
**Step 7:** Other tips and suggestions:
- Always have brochures or information regarding your rental with you.
- Do what you can but don't hesitate to hire a professional.
- Get a copy of the rental contract and go over it.
- Start small and don't take on more than you can handle.
- Keep the guests' perspective in view at all times.

*"It's kind of fun to do the impossible."*
                                    -Walt Disney

# APPENDIX E

### ONLINE MARKETING AND SOCIAL MEDIA FOR PROPERTY MANAGEMENT
by Trevor Henson

**Where We Started and Where We Are Going**

Property Management has been around as long as people have been investing in real estate itself. Our industry has been leasing and managing spaces for people to lay their heads since the first wealthy merchants invested in apartments and stores in cities far from their homes or farms. These merchants inevitably needed a trusted businessman to collect rent and keep an eye on their investments – thus, the property management industry was born.

The maturity of the property management industry gives us a solid foundation of procedures, laws, ethics and marketing tactics (log onto **NAA.org** or **IREM.org** for more info). Of all the real estate camps, property management is the most traditional brick and mortar business. We commonly perceive ourselves as not in need of the Internet or technology to collect rent checks, place "For Rent" signs, answer phones or send maintenance personnel to fix a leak. Furthermore, our clients (owners and investors) find us through advertisements in trade magazines, direct mail campaigns or referrals from brokers. Why should we as property management professionals worry about things such as online marketing and social media such as Facebook and Twitter? Why should we invest an immeasurable amount of time into a medium that will presumably fade out? **Because the way our customers and prospects do business is *changing*.**

**Your Apartment Guide Better Have Dot Com on the End**

A 2007 study conducted by Pew Internet & American Life Project (www.**pewinternet**.org) indicates that almost half of those searching for a new place to live start their search on the Internet. More importantly, the study points out that prospects use the Internet *just as frequently* as they use print media to begin their search for a new home or apartment.

| What people do when they start the process of looking for a place to live | |
|---|---|
| Use the Internet | 49% |
| Look through newspapers for ads and articles | 49 |
| Ask a real estate agent for advice | 47 |
| Ask friends, family members, or co-workers | 31 |
| Use another source not mentioned already | 17 |
| Use television and radio | 15 |

**Source:** *Pew Internet & American Life Project Survey, September 2007, n=314 for those who found a new place to live in prior year, margin of error is ±6%.*

In addition, the use of social media networks such as Facebook, Twitter and LinkedIn has doubled since 2007, according to a report from Forrester Research (check out **http://mashable.com/2009/07/28/social-networking-users-us** for the full article). The report states that approximately 55.6 million adults in the United States – just less than one-third of the population – currently visit social media networks.

What does this tell the property management industry? It screams to us that online marketing and social media cannot and will not be ignored. If 49% of our rental prospects are using the Internet as a primary or secondary source to find us, then we owe it to our clients and ourselves to keep up with the trending technology.

### A Prospect Recruited Online Makes a Great Tenant

At First Light Property Management, we have found that prospects who contact us from an online vacancy posting turn into excellent tenants. These tenants generally prefer to communicate via email, submit their applications online, submit maintenance requests online, and pay rent through their online tenant accounts. These options help our company become more efficient, effectively lowering overhead and allowing us to pass better prices on to our owners.

Below is a quick example from one of our marketing campaigns that advertised vacancies in the San Diego area to returning servicemen onboard Navy ships.

Our residence manager, Julie, received word that a Navy aircraft carrier was returning from service in the Middle East, carrying with it 5,000+ servicemen and women. She concluded that the service people would most certainly be in need of housing and that not everyone returning home would want to live on the Navy base. This was an opportunity for Julie to potentially fill a few vacancies with high quality tenants – but what was the best approach?

After carefully assessing the details, Julie sent an email to the ship's public affairs liaison officer, asking if any of his sailors would need help finding civilian housing upon return to the United States. She said if the officer would simply forward the housing information to the ship, she would give a 15% discount on monthly rent to any of the seamen that contacted her. Julie also explained that the entire application and leasing process would be handled via email and through the website. This approach was seen very favorably by the Navy as their sailors had very limited access to phones while onboard, but had plenty of Internet access to communicate via email.

The result of Julie's efforts to contact the Navy at an opportune time, combined with the established online tenant application and rental process, allowed for successful placements of quality tenants, tenants who, a year later, not only consistently paid their rent on time, but submitted maintenance requests and questions via email without unnecessarily involving the residence manager.

As we can see, this is just one creative example of effectively reaching your web-based audience. There are many online tools available that can lend your property management company a hand in accessing digital prospects, tenants, and clients. If your company has the patience and resources to move its database online, then it is well worth the time and investment. Landlords can enjoy the total essence of transparent accounting, even having the capability of knowing to the minute which tenants have paid their rent for the month, all the while monitoring work order submittals, status and completions. There are many ways to set up a web-based property management system, but the easiest are pre-built online programs, such as **AppFolio.com** or **Buildium.com**.

**Where to Begin: "Traditional" Online Marketing**

The absolute first thing that a property management company must do before entering the web marketing and social media arena is to define its target markets and set measurable goals. There are entire books written on these subjects and it is beyond the scope of this discussion. Check out *The New Rules of Marketing and PR* by David Meerman Scott. Pay special attention to Chapter 10, for a good starting point on information regarding marketing plans and organizational goals.

The next step is to research web marketing options and decide which online tools will be the most effective in helping your company achieve the goals set forth.

To begin, let's talk about the more "traditional" online tools available for increasing your company's web presence. These tools include advertising on apartment websites and a website for your company. We will then move into a discussion on social media known by many as *Web 2.0*. For those new to the term, **Wikipedia** defines Web 2.0 very accurately:

> "A Web 2.0 site allows its users to interact with other users or to change website content, in contrast to non-interactive websites where users are limited to the passive viewing of information that is provided to them." (wikipedia.org/wiki/Web_2.0)

**Internet Listing Services**

Internet Listing Services (ILS) primarily target prospective tenants through websites that cater to apartment and home seekers. The largest and most successful ILS in your area will consistently rank in the top 10 keyword searches, for example, "apartments in Los Angeles," or "apartments for rent."

There are three general types of ILS: Pay-per-lead, pay-per-listing, and free listing. Below is a clarification on how these pricing structures work:

*Pay-per-lead:* The property management company pays for each email or phone lead that comes into the leasing office. Example: **Rent.com**

*Pay-per-listing:* The property management company pays a monthly flat-rate fee to advertise a specific apartment listing and/or floor plan. Examples: **Move.com** and **Apartments.com**

*Free listings:* The property management company incurs no cost to post vacancies. These types of sites generally drive the most traffic, but require the most user maintenance (e.g.

frequent updates from property management staff). Examples: **Westsiderentals.com**, **Kijiji.com**, and **4rentinla.com**

Search Google and Bing for the ILS in your area that would most likely show up first in a prospective tenant's browser, and post vacancies accordingly.

**Current Listings Web Page**

One of the best ways to provide prospective tenants current vacancy information is to have a page on your company website dedicated to "Available Units" or "Current Listings" (a simple tab on your navigation bar or link on your home page will help). The page itself does not need to be flashy or fancy – just simple and up-to-date. It is here where images, unit addresses, floor plans, video walk-throughs, move-in specials, and all unit and community information should be listed. The page should be updated as frequently as needed in order to reflect changes in offered rents, availability, etc.

**Moving Up: Social Media for the Property Management Company**

Taking one more step, the world of Web 2.0 and social media allows you as a company to directly interface with potential tenants, investors, and clients. Social media is a vast universe and all of the reading, digesting and commenting on articles, blogs, tweets, lenses (see **Squidoo.com**), etc. could become a full-time job! There are dozens of books and websites on social media and online marketing, however, we have found the following options to be successful tactics for helping to drive web traffic to a home page and establish credibility within the field.

Each of the following social media outlets can be used in an infinite amount of combinations, utilizing a slew of add-on applications, widgets and third-party vendors. It is important to keep in mind that with social media there is no *right* way to use it – just be honest and find out what works for your particular company. If you are absolutely new to the concept and culture of social media as a whole, I suggest reading *Trust Agents* by Chris Brogan and Julien Smith. Brogan and Smith's book breaks the industry down in a language that everyone can relate to. We highly recommend it.

**Blogs:** If you have anything to say at all about the property management industry, a blog is the place to speak your mind. Perhaps you or your company has an out-of-the-box method of marketing your vacancies? We would love to hear about it. Hard week in the rental office? We want to know about that too. Or maybe you have insight on an old dilemma and need a sounding board? Your blog is the place to do it. To create your own, check out **typepad.com** or **wordpress.com**. The sites will walk you through all the setup. One key point to remember when writing your blog: include pictures! Everyone enjoys a little color and imagery during the digestion of news topics.

Additionally, there are online networking sites that allow you to post your blog as well as start and/or participate in discussion groups. The strongest and most notable in the property management and multifamily industry is **MultifamilyInsiders.com**. Created and managed by Brent Williams, Multifamily Insiders is an excellent place to share your knowledge and experiences in the industry.

**Twitter:** Twitter is considered a micro-blogging tool. We use it to get up-to-the-minute property management news by following other users who have their fingers on the pulse of the industry, as well as to advertise units, open houses, and move-in specials. There is a host of uses for Twitter, but it is best summed up by John Jantsch, founder of Duct Tape Marketing (**www.ducttapemarketing.com**):

*"(1) I get great insight when I ask questions, (2) let's face it, I get traffic and (3) people on Twitter spread my thoughts to new places."*

It is very simple to create a Twitter profile at **Twitter.com** and start following other users and companies you find interesting. For more info, check out: **http://business.twitter.com/twitter101**

**Facebook Fan Page:** The Fan Page provides your company with another space to share information. Our company's Twitter and blog feeds are connected to our Fan Page so that each time we post a new blog or tweet, it immediately posts to First Light's Fan Page. Even if you start out with a small fan following (friends, relatives, vendors, etc.), your company information is available to the 350+ million users on Facebook. This results in increased traffic to your website.

I am often asked: "What's the point of social media, really?" The point is a measured increase in website traffic coupled with educated conversations about technology and developments in the property management industry. These conversations ultimately garner real world insight that allows us to intelligently communicate with owners, tenants, and prospects alike. But please do not take my word for it, the chart on the following page tells the story of how real estate is being found by our audience.

| Online tools used by those who use the Internet in their search for a place to live | |
|---|---|
| Take a video tour or virtual tour of a house, apartment, or neighborhood | 54% |
| FInd information online about the quality of life in a community | 51 |
| Search websites of real estate companies and agents | 50 |
| Search newspaper ads online | 42 |
| Search online ad sites such as Craig's list | 32 |
| Read blogs about the community | 24 |
| Post or read messages in chat rooms, listservs, or other online forums | 19 |

**Source:** *Pew Internet & American Life Project Survey, September 2007, n=152 for those who used the Internet in their research into finding a new place to live; margin of error is ±9%.*

Although our wealthy merchant of ancient days had no idea that an entire industry could spring from the simple idea of renting a home or a store, it is fair to assume that finding a tenant was equally important to him as it is to us in 2010. The difference, now, is in the means by which the advertising message is delivered. Typically the messages in property management have been delivered by hand, phone, or newsprint, but we now must consider the alternatives. Online venues and social media outlets can and will change, but the premise is clear: our customers want to interact and participate with us, not just read and consume information. So log in, blog out and tweet up. The conversation is only beginning and the property management industry is no exception to dialogue.

# ABOUT THE AUTHOR

Michael Levy worked for Hewlett-Packard (HP) for 25+ years in various jobs including software R&D, information technology, product marketing, quality, and manufacturing positions. When Michael left HP in 2002, he started a consulting business focused on helping real estate professionals use technology to help improve their bottom line results.

In 2003, Michael co-founded NorthernColoradoRentals.com, now the largest rental listing website in Northern Colorado. A few years later, in 2008, Michael co-founded NoCoAds, a local advertising network that allows Northern Colorado businesses to do targeted advertising for a fraction of the cost of traditional advertising. In 2009, Michael began work on his first book, *50 Interviews: Successful Property Managers*.

Michael graduated from the University of California, San Diego (UCSD), with a degree in applied physics and information science. Michael also has a master of business administration (M.B.A.), with an emphasis in computer systems, from the University of California, Los Angeles (UCLA).

Michael was an executive level software R&D lab manager most recently with HP, where he made substantial contributions in the area of new product development. Michael managed up to 100 engineers and their managers, and a $15M annual budget. He has a proven track record of industry leading new product development, from inception to product release. Michael successfully managed the development of multiple releases of many of HP's most successful software products.

Michael also has 16 years of international management experience, including four years working in Bristol, England where he managed an IT organization of over 100 engineers and managers responsible for the development and support of all the IT systems for a customer support business unit in EMEA[1]. While in Bristol, Michael led the effort to implement a new software development methodology within the organization using a very effective management of change (MOC) process.

[1] *EMEA: Europe, the Middle East and Africa.*

# ABOUT 50 INTERVIEWS

Imagine a university where not only does each student get a text book custom tailored to a curriculum they personally designed, but where each student literally becomes the author!

The mission of 50 Interviews, Inc. is to provide aspiring, passionate, driven people a framework to achieve their dreams of becoming that which they aspire to be. Learning what it takes to be the best in your field; directly from those who have already succeeded. The ideal author is someone who desires to be a recognized expert in their field. You will be part of a community of authors who share your passion and who have learned firsthand how the **50 Interviews** concept works. A form of extreme education, the process will transform you into that which you aspire to become.

50 Interviews is a publisher of books, CDs, videos, and software that serve to inform, educate, and inspire others on a wide range of topics. Timely insight, inspiration, collective wisdom, and best practices derived directly from those who have already succeeded. Authors surround themselves with those they admire, gain clarity of purpose, adopt critical beliefs, and build a network of peers to ensure success in that endeavor. Readers gain knowledge and perspective from those who have already achieved a result they desire.

If you are intersted in learning more, I would love to hear from you! You can contact me via email at: brian@50interviews.com, by phone: 970-215-1078 (Colorado), or through our website:

## www.50interviews.com

All my best,
Brian Schwartz
Authorpreneur and creator of **50 Interviews**

# OTHER 50 INTERVIEWS TITLES

Additional topics based on the *50 Interviews* model that have already been released or are in development:

**Successful Property Managers (Volume 1)**
*by Michael Levy*

**Successful Jobseekers**
*by Gordon Nuttall*

**Young Entrepreneurs**
*by Nick Tart*

**Artists**
*by Maryann Swartz*

**Video Marketers**
*by Randy Berry*

**Attraction Marketers**
*by Rob Christensen*

**Spiritualists**
*by Tuula Fai*

**Athletes over 50**
*by Don McGrath*

**Scientists**
*by David Giltner*

**Wealth Managers**
*by Allen Duck*

**Direct Sales**
*by Kirsten McCay-Smith*

**Entrepreneurs**
*by Brian Schwartz*

**Professional Speakers**
*by Laura Lee Carter and Brian Schwartz*

Learn more at
**www.50interviews.com**

www.ingramcontent.com/pod-product-compliance
Lightning Source LLC
Chambersburg PA
CBHW030324080526
44584CB00012B/695